Making your business less dependent on YOU

By the founder of A4G
(a company with over 30 years of uninterrupted growth)
and Author of *Accidental Millionaires*

MALCOLM PALMER

Acknowledgements

Many thanks to my hard-working proof-reader Holly White for all the corrections and suggestions she made but most importantly for allowing me to break a few grammatical rules in order to emphasise a few points.

And a big thank you to Ayse Cooper for all her hard work promoting this book and for all the research on this project leading up to publication.

But most of all, thank you to all my clients. I have witnessed all your hard work and the challenges you have faced, day in day out. I am proud to have been part of your journey. Your dedication to your businesses, your staff and your customers and the ingenuity and drive you demonstrate every day are my inspiration for the book.

"There were parts of this book that felt they were written about me! The situations, the issues and the relationships with family and staff. Great content for anyone who feels their business is too dependent on them"

John Skudder, Skuddair ltd

Contents

Foreward   **VIII**

Section A   The problem   **1**
Chapter 1 – Life on the doughnut   3
Chapter 2 – So much to do, so little time   9
Chapter 3 – Are you the only person who can do this job?   13
Chapter 4 – At least the Ford was paid for   19
Chapter 5 – Are you a Ronald or an Elton?   25
Chapter 6 – Pause for thought   31

Section B   Taking control
Chapter 7 – Silver spoon or balls of steel   37
Chapter 8 – If only they all had the same attitude as Phil   43
Chapter 9 – What next?   49
Chapter 10 – It's all about "levewage"   57
Chapter 11 – Set the hares running   65
Chapter 12 – Outcome, Performance, Process   71
Chapter 13 – The Moneyball concept   75
Chapter 14 – Sliding doors   81
Chapter 15 – Finding your invisible heroes   87
Chapter 16 – Mr Leverage and Mr Systems   91

Section C   Boring is under-rated

Chapter 17 – Sloping shoulders and monkey collectors	99
Chapter 18 – Systems and admin	105
Chapter 19 – Are we human or are we dancers?	111
Chapter 20 – A helping non-human hand	117
Chapter 21 – The three reasons things go wrong	123
Chapter 22 – The muddy bit in the middle	131

Section D   The light at the end of the tunnel

Chapter 23 – Growing pains	138
Chapter 24 – The man in the bowler hat	145
Chapter 25 – Good arguments and bad arguments	151
Chapter 26 – Leading from the back	155
Chapter 27 – Some me time	161
Chapter 28 – Succession	169
Chapter 29 – Reaching the promised land	177

Next steps	**185**
Appendix A – Example Staff page	188
Appendix B – Example Index of roles	189
Appendix C – Example role page	191
Appendix D – Example of standard system	192
A4G Breakthrough Freedom Programme	195
References	201

Foreword

1st March 2025. Big day.

As I write this, we haven't reached that day yet. But as you read this (unless you're the proof-reader), that day has now passed.

"Why is it a big day?" I hear you ask.

Well first of all it's the 30th anniversary of the day I started.

But more significantly, it's the day we have all agreed from which I shall no longer be Managing Partner of my accounting practice, A4G.

Whilst it sounds like a big step, it's not really. We've been working towards this day for years.

In reality, we've been sharing responsibilities for a number of years. And we'll be sharing them afterwards as well.

It's just that the buck won't stop with me.

Foreword

I'm not retiring. God forbid. I love working with clients, I love working with a team that I've watched grow up, I love tinkering with systems and processes, training staff, helping people grow.

But 1st March is a key date. Because the business is no longer dependent on me.

30 years of continuous growth. Sometimes two steps forward, one step back, but always progress.

In my last book, Accidental Millionaires, I examined the mindset that results in people going from a one-person business to a success story. Even if the owners of those businesses don't even realise they have that mindset.

And what all *Accidental Millionaires* know is that what got you here, won't get you there. Change is inevitable. As your business grows you risk becoming a prisoner of your own success with a business that struggles to function without you.

So that's my motivation for this book. To help you make your business less dependent on you.

Section A
The problem

Life on the doughnut

So, where are you right now?

It's an interesting question, isn't it? Because there's two ways of answering that.

There is the physical sense of course. 'Well, I'm sitting in a traffic jam on the motorway looking at my emails to use the time productively.'

Or there's the mental sense. 'yeah, pretty good. Maybe a bit stressed about a few things.'

For many of you when you get home tonight, you'll be asked by a loved one or friend whether today was "a good day at the office". But what makes it a good day and what makes it a bad day?

A good way of visualising it is thinking about all the possible mental states as being somewhere on a round doughnut - the ones with a hole in the middle like the one in the picture.

The hole in the middle is when you're reading a book, sleeping, watching

Chapter 1

TV or whatever your way of relaxing is.

The bit outside the doughnut is when you're out of control. Maybe in a good way like an intense sports match (playing or maybe for some of us just supporting). But perhaps in a bad way when your emotions have overtaken the logical part of your brain and you're upset, angry or worse.

The rest of the time your mental state and your conscious brain is somewhere on the doughnut. Hopefully, you are somewhere on the doughnut at all times in the working day.

In my accountancy practice, we once had someone here on work experience who fell asleep in the toilets for several hours. We called his college and home to alert them to a missing teenager. And then he just strolled back into the office as if nothing had happened.

We also made the mistake one year of having the office party in the middle of the week. The following day, one staff member (who is now a partner I might add) had to go and have a doze in the staff room.

Other than that, I can't think of many times when someone has been in the hole in the middle of the doughnut during the working day.

Occasionally one or two people get close and we have had the occasional meltdown when someone is outside the doughnut and feeling overwhelmed about a problem or workload but fortunately we have some pretty good team leaders who can gee things up a bit.

But this isn't about my staff or even your staff for that matter.

It's about you. In fact, this whole book is about you.

So, where's the ideal place to be? Near the middle? Nice and relaxed, sailing round the office with chirpy conversation, uplifting the team as you ponder what on earth you're going to do when you finally make it to your desk because you have so few responsibilities these days?

Chapter 1

I doubt it.

That's not you, is it? Not if you are the person who set this business up in the first place and worked 15-hour days to get it all to where it is now. Not if you still have a hunger for the business to be more than it currently is. Not if your competitive instincts want you to keep growing even if the part of you that likes your holidays and off time is constantly asking you questions about how hard you work.

So you're on the doughnut. And probably not near the middle. More likely nearer the edge. Maybe only a step or two away from being outside the doughnut out of control, in crisis-mode.

You probably feel that you need to lead from the front. If you're not the one driving and pushing, who else will?

One of the team and I used to refer to a now ex-colleague as Levi because he was always out the door at 5.01. He assiduously avoided moving too far away from the middle of the doughnut.

Of course, the problem with that was that it pushed other people closer to the edge of their particular doughnut. When he dodged anything urgent, someone else had to do it.

Personally, I'd rather be closer to the edge than the middle. But not too close.

We all have times when we drift a bit close to the edge. When you're in the thick of that huge contract you signed which is starting to go wrong. When you've got lots of great work on the go, but a legal dispute has arisen in relation to another job or maybe with an employee.

Add in a few personal or family things and your usual positive demeanour is replaced by a grumpy boss who is snappy with their team and a team who don't understand why.

It's possible that you are your own worst enemy on that front. When

Chapter 1

you're on top of things, what do you get drawn to do? Important but not urgent tasks that will make the business less dependent on you when it gets busy again? Or are you drawn to a new project, another business deal, more aggressive marketing and sales?

That's not to say that the latter approach is wrong. It depends where you are and where you want to be. Sometimes it's a fine line between boredom and stress!

Here's the big problem. Here's the paradox of this situation and probably the reason why you aren't doing anything about it.

The problem is that when you are stretched like this, you are also at your most profitable. Everyone is running at full pelt. There's no slack in the system but there's a lot of energy.

So your profits are going up which is good, right?

But that makes it very hard to contemplate that there's a problem. Worse, you're also at your most vulnerable to a mistake.

In the early years of my career, I acted for a printing company who went through two years of extraordinary growth. Lots of new staff, changes of premises, on the edge of their cash flow all the time.

Back then, all printers were using what were relatively new Apple Macs. These were expensive but there was a shortfall. Apple couldn't make them fast enough. As a result, there was a second-hand market where machines were being sold for more than cost.

One day they came into the office and there had been a burglary. All the Apple Macs had been stolen. The police said that it was targeted.

They called the insurance company and the assessor visited within 24 hours. "Where's your Redcare alarm system?" he said.

"Oh, it was due to be installed next week" was the reply.

Chapter 1

"In that case you're not insured" replied the assessor.

That was it. Game over. With no spare resources to replace their expensive equipment, the company could not trade and went into liquidation.

They'd just been too busy to get something essential done.

If you're feeling close to the edge of your own particular doughnut, it's important to rationalise it and think why that might be. There are lots of reasons:

- It might be temporary. Those manic days that fly by dealing with one big problem or lots of little ones can be fun. But if there are too many of them, that can lead to burnout.

- You've simply got too many responsibilities. If that's the case, you need some solutions. That's one of the aims of this book. There's always a solution in the long run. But it needs to be the right one.

- Maybe there are things on your plate that weren't as important or urgent as you thought they were or as urgent. Maybe we can delegate some of them away.

- You're not as close to the edge as you think but you are just beating yourself up over not being able to do everything. This is sometimes referred to as 'Imposter Syndrome' but it's also caused by the emotional side of your brain (the back bit) drowning out the logical side (the front bit). This is explored in an excellent book called 'The Chimp Paradox' by Dr Steve Peters.

- Your job is far more complicated than it needs to be and maybe a bit of a systems overhaul is needed.

Alternatively, perhaps someone else is pushing you closer to the edge of your doughnut than you would be if they were doing their job properly. Handle this one with care though. They may be closer to the edge of their

Chapter 1

own personal doughnut than you realise.

Or maybe they're closer to the hole in the middle than you realise. Maybe they're capable of a lot more than you think. A constant goal for you as leader of your organisation should be try and identify unfulfilled talent. I always believe people are capable of personal growth, sometimes when they don't even think it themselves!

So, will today be a good day at the office?

Well, we don't know the answer to that for certain do we? Problems may occur that you couldn't have predicted at the start of the day.

If an average day is spent on the outer limits of the doughnut, then your business is far too dependent on you.

Let's get this journey started.

Chapter 2

So much to do, so little time

"God, what a day." thought David Bright as he noticed the time on the office clock.

"6.40", he thought, "I'll only be 15 minutes late if I get everything shut down and locked up quickly." Home by 7 o'clock had been his New Year's resolution or at least the New Year's resolution imposed on him by his wife, Jean.

A month in and he'd never missed it by more than half an hour. "How many other people have kept their New Year's resolution by the end of January?" he thought – ignoring the fact that he was now going to bed an hour early and setting the alarm an hour early to get into the office an hour earlier every day.

He glanced at his inbox. 58 emails. This morning there had been 59. A whole day mostly spent in the office, and he'd only answered one email.

Of course, that wasn't the case; he'd actually answered about a hundred but another ninety-nine had taken their place. "Well, at least it's progress." he mumbled to himself. David Bright had always been a glass is half-full

Chapter 2

kind of man. Of course, the two emails that would arrive that night; one about an order from China and the other from a customer who was always sending out emails into the small hours meant that by 9am he would be up to 60.

As the computer shut down and the glow disappeared from the office's fluorescent lights the realisation suddenly dawned on him that he'd forgotten something.

The delivery note for the job at Callums'. If he didn't get that ready, the fitters would end up spending the first two hours of the day arguing about where they should begin and John McDonald (probably his least favourite customer) would probably try and use the unsigned, key piece of paperwork as an excuse for a debate about the standard of the work which was basically a tactic for trying to knock something off the pre-agreed price.

David wondered whether he could get in early to get it completed but he knew that wasn't going to happen.

Perhaps he could email it to Gary (his most reliable employee) who could print it off and drive to Callums' premises to get it signed in the morning.

Yes, that's the answer thought David as he typed 75135 into the alarm code and heard the satisfying bleep of the alarm that always signalled the end of a working day and the start of the journey home. Click went the security shutters then the door lock as he braced himself against the cold for a few seconds before unlocking his car.

He started the engine, heard the familiar tones of his favourite radio presenter, turned the heater in the car up and the de-mister on. Then he remembered. Bugger he thought. "The funeral."

Tomorrow morning was Peter Lamb's funeral.

Peter Lamb ran Awesome Despatch, a same day and overnight delivery company that Bright Interiors regularly used to take specialist IT and

Chapter 2

office equipment to sites that they were working on.

For a few fleeting seconds he wondered whether he could perhaps miss the funeral, but Peter was one of David's longest standing business acquaintances and as close to a friend that David had in business. Peter had dug David out of a few spots over the years and even lent him ten grand when things were tight.

"Jean," said David on his mobile phone. "I think I'm about to break my New Year's resolution."

Back at Hollywell, The Street, Cobdown a familiar scene was about to be played out. "Hungry?" said Jean Bright to her youngest child Ruby.

"Why?" asked Ruby slowly, her privately educated accent hanging on the "Y" part of why in the way that someone does when they know the answer already. "Because there are two dinners to eat if you want them." replied her mother.

Ruby was pretty used to this particular scenario.

Both of her elder brothers had left home years before and in fact so had she for eleven weeks, three times a year as she got her 2.1 in history down on the south coast. But this time was different and not because it was the first time since New Year's Eve that it had happened.

This time was different because she'd really wanted to sit and have a chat about what she was doing the following day. Her new job at Abrahams and Co, the firm that had been Dad's accountants for so many years.

Dinner was eaten with relatively few words. Mum was great but career advice had never been her thing.

Ruby inhaled her food the way that the youngest of three siblings always does when childhood meals have been spent trying to fend off two elder brothers determined to steal her dinner and then headed upstairs for an evening on Instagram and TikTok.

Chapter 3

Are you the only person who can do this job?

In my book *Accidental Millionaires*, I outlined the strategic planning process in Chapter 4. If you want to read it in full, you can do so by going onto my website www.malcolm-palmer.com But if you haven't read it, there are five key stages:

1. Where you want to be in (say) 3 years' time?
2. Where are you now?
3. What Key Performance Indicators (KPIs) do you need to hit to get from where you are now to where you want to be?
4. What actions will you need to take to hit those KPIs?
5. What will stop you?

Most business coaches (even the really good ones) spend most of their time focussing on the 4th part of that equation; the action plan.

That works with a lot of business owners. But many business owners fall away from the plan very quickly because 'events' take over. Someone leaves. The order book looks a bit low, and they need to rustle up some business. The contracts manager they took on isn't quite as good as their CV (or their interview) suggested. Materials prices increase as a result of

Chapter 3

some world event that no-one could have predicted, and belts now need be tightened.

These are the things that will stop you i.e. point 5!

The reality is that if you're honest about it, this business is far too dependent on you.

So, for each task you have on today, you need to ask yourself:

'Are you the only person that can do this job?'

I once got asked that by a very wise business mentor.

He wasn't talking about my actual job. What he was telling me was that I should have a sign on my desk that said that to challenge myself about every task that I was doing.

Human beings are creatures of habit. We must be, otherwise we would hardly get anything done. Imagine if every single day, you had to think of a different way to get out of bed, a different place to brush your teeth, a new and exciting breakfast that you'd never had before.

David Attenborough often gets asked about why he always wears the same clothes. Beige slacks and pale blue shirt, in case you're wondering. One reason is that it helps with continuity so that if they have to re-film anything, he's always wearing the same thing.

Equally, it's one less thing for him to think about. Consider all the knowledge that he's got about the planet, animals and creatures that live now or millions of years ago. That's a lot of knowledge and a lot of head space. There's one less thing to think about if you don't have to worry about what you're going to wear.

As our businesses grow, so does our frustration with the inability of everyone around us to think like we do.

Chapter 3

The (unrealistic) dream is that we will find mini versions of us, who can automatically think like we do and act in our interests.

But constantly looking for a person like that is a thankless task.

If you ever find them, then hang onto them as long as possible because there's no guarantee that they are going to be around forever.

It's possible that just at the point you feel they are doing the job the way you want them to do it, they will get headhunted by a competitor for more than you can afford to pay them.

Or they may go off and set up their own company. Just like you did.

So, unless hope is a huge part of strategy, then you are going to have to have a re-think.

Let's go back to when you started the business. How long did it take you until your week was full? A few months? A couple of years? Maybe you were pretty good at taking on staff at the right time to enable the business to grow.

Without realising it, your management style evolved. It may have been based on the things you learned from those who managed you. Or perhaps it was based on trying to do everything in a different way to some of the hopeless bosses you had in the past. Maybe it just evolved based on trial and error and the things you learnt as you went on, with a little bit of your own personal principles (and sometimes prejudices) thrown in.

Whatever that style is, sooner or later the business will find itself on a bit of a plateau.

Every business has a natural plateau to it but without adapting your style you will never get off that plateau.

The first step is that you must learn to trust other people. Within reason.

Chapter 3

A lot of business owners really struggle with this. They know they need some help but the thought of getting that from someone they don't know, fills them with dread. Sometimes they just stick as they are as a one man or woman business. Much less trouble that way!

Sometimes they carry this around with them until an opportunity presents itself. A friend is unhappy in their job, or a family member becomes unemployed. "What about coming to work for me?" they say.

Occasionally this works. But it's a road full of jeopardy.

A friend of mine from college took on his best friend as a salesman. These guys had been best men for each other at their respective weddings. Six months after one started work for the other, they fell out and have never spoken again.

As parents, we are always worried about our children and always looking for ways to help them. Situations in their lives arise where we think we can help them and ourselves by giving them a job.

There are advantages of this. Hopefully they care for us as people more than our employees do. Hopefully!

But of course, they come with baggage - namely their relationship with us. They might not take a job with us as seriously as they would take a job with someone else. They might not take kindly to us telling them what to do or what they did wrong. If it's our kids, we may find ourselves re-enacting conversations from their teenage years that we thought were in the past!

There are lots of people out there who can help you though. Yes, we know the UK job market makes it hard to find staff at the moment but if you look hard enough you will find them. That might require you to recruit offshore (but we'll get to that later).

You've probably been on management courses. If you're reading this book, you've probably read other books. The one-minute manager by

Chapter 3

Spencer Blanchard is a great book to help you with that journey from taking on a new employee to them being someone you can trust to get on with their job with very little input from you.

But you've got to be prepared to make that journey.

You are? Great, let's keep going then.

Chapter 4

At least the Ford was paid for

The following morning Ruby was awake early worrying about making a good first impression.

"I know this is what I really want to do." She muttered, trying to convince herself more than anything else. Downstairs, her father was already up and about.

"Morning Dad!" said Ruby eagerly waiting his first question but none came. "Are you going to a funeral?" asked Ruby suddenly noticing the black tie and suit her father was wearing. "Peter's" came the slightly distracted reply.

"Peter who?" said Ruby searching her memory for all the Peters she knew who might have died recently.

"Peter Lamb" came the reply.

Still nothing.

Chapter 4

"Peter Lamb, owner of Awesome Despatch. Used to come to the New Year's Eve party until he split up with his first wife." Said David impatiently. Nothing again.

How can the daughter who lives in the same house as me and who even worked with me for a few months not have heard of one of my closest friends? thought David.

"Friends? Blimey, someone I've haven't socialised with for years has become one of my closest friends." Then he noticed the blouse and smart fitted trousers his daughter was wearing. *She looks smart thought David who wasn't used to seeing his youngest child or any of them for that matter, wearing any other than scruffy tee-shirts and torn jeans.*

They left at the same time. One in a brand-new Tesla and the other in a clapped-out Ford. At least the Ford was paid for though.

Forty-five minutes later with the small Ford safely parked in the office car park, Ruby Bright was face to face with Matt Pevy, her new boss.

After the usual pleasantries had been exchanged, Matt and Ruby sat down to run through Ruby's induction programme.

Ruby tried to recall the details of the induction programme from her first day at Bright Interiors five months earlier, but the memory was sketchy and had possibly been concluded after James Stanmore, Bright Interiors' then resident moaner and cynic had wafted his hand in the general direction of the ladies' toilets and the metal stairs that led up to 'the office wallahs'.

"OK, first things first, Ruby. Akram was really impressed with you and said he thought you'd go far. He reckons you think that we've all got a pretty easy life here though?"

"Well, it was only what Dad told me. He reckons accountants have got it made. Earn loads of money and swan off to the golf course or pub whenever they feel like it. Sounded pretty good to me!"

Chapter 4

"Yeah, that sounds like your Dad. He loves pulling my leg about that one. OK well I don't want to disillusion you on your first day, but passing your exams isn't a passport to guaranteed riches you know. That's what I always thought while I was training. I started with a firm called Levington Phillips and Bruce."

The blank look confirmed that Ruby had never heard of them. "You won't have heard of them because they got swallowed up when Nicholas Levington decided to retire, and the other partners couldn't afford to buy him out." Said Matt. "They were ok to train with, but a bit old school if you know what I mean."

"Old school?" queried Ruby.

"Yeah, they just bashed out accounts and tax returns and didn't give any advice. Most firms were like that back then though.

When I got nearer to qualifying, I started to see how hard all the partners worked. They were in early, left late and even visited clients in the evening and at weekends. They all drove nice cars, but I wasn't sure whether the rewards they were getting, were worth all the work they were putting in."

"Sounds like Uncle Eric"

"Who's Uncle Eric?"

"You know Eric. You took over his business."

"Oh sorry, Eric Abrahams. Uncle Eric? I didn't know you were related."

"We're not" Ruby replied." We used to call all our Mum and Dad's friends Auntie and Uncle. It was only a few years ago I even realised he was Dad's accountant."

"Yeah. Poor old Uncle Eric. Eric and Kitty used to come to the annual New Year's Eve party, and he'd lecture me about passing my exams and getting

Chapter 4

into a stable profession. Dad didn't want me to come into the family business and thought Uncle Eric would take me into his firm to 'do my articles' whatever they were. I was always a bit scared of him when I was little because he always wore these funny waistcoats and peered over the top of his half-rimmed specs but once I got to know him, I realised he was alright really."

"Bit of a shock when he died?" asked Matt.

"Yeah, Dad was really cut up. Mum too. There were loads of people at the funeral though. His four sons all had one of his favourite waistcoats on. All his clients were telling stories about nights out they'd had with him. He was a bit of a character." Said Ruby as the thought suddenly dawned on her that Dad was off to the funeral of another business acquaintance who apparently hadn't made it to retirement.

"When I qualified, there weren't too many jobs around and even though Levington Philips and Bruce seemed to be going nowhere, I was stuck." Smiled Matt enjoying the nostalgic stories of his new employee. "I was a bit of a boy-racer in those days and a change of career with a lower salary wasn't a particularly attractive option. Then I was at a tax seminar, and I got chatting to a nice lady who said she had work coming out of her ears and that her firm was looking for someone to help. Next thing I know, she'd booked up an interview with her firm Mortimore & Co."

"I've never heard of them either I'm afraid." said Ruby suddenly wondering if perhaps she ought to have learnt a little more about the profession he was now entering.

"Oh sorry, I should explain, Ron Mortimore was a competitor of Levingtons. My old boss hated him. Said he was a cowboy because he kept taking clients off us by being cheaper. Strangest interview I ever had. I was worried about being ten minutes late because of the traffic but when I got there the secretary said he wasn't in and didn't know anything about an interview. They eventually tracked him down to a client's office and he said he'd forgotten all about it. I went back the following day, and he was so apologetic about forgetting the interview that I just sailed through. It

Chapter 4

was more like I was interviewing him, apart from when we kept getting interrupted by urgent phone calls that only he could deal with."

"A bit disorganised then?"

"He was. I was tempted to sneak out when he was on one of these phone calls and run as fast as I could, but I wanted to find out why he kept nicking clients off us. And he had so much work that when he offered me a job with a pay increase, I just thought it was too good an opportunity to miss."

"Wasn't he just under-cutting everyone else on price?"

"No, it was more complicated than that. He charged the same hourly rates as everyone else, but he just got everything done much quicker."

"Why was that?"

"Well, mainly, Ron had cut out all sorts of review processes and just simplified the way that all the accounts were done. Get it in, get it done, get it out and get it billed – that was his motto. It was a real culture shock at the time."

"Didn't you get loads of things go wrong?"

"Sometimes, but not any more than we had at Levingtons.

It was like everyone took responsibility at Mortimore's and didn't make many mistakes. At Levingtons, if they made a mistake, they said that the manager should have picked it up. They just didn't care. At Mortimore's though, we were flying by the seat of our pants all the time but we all just mucked in. Clients would come in and end up seeing juniors sometimes, but they got a good service at a good price and didn't seem to mind too much. Besides, most of the juniors were pretty good, once they knew what was what. As long as it got done, most of the clients didn't mind."

Chapter 4

"So you were all good delegators then?"

"We didn't have much choice. We wouldn't have got the work out otherwise. Ron always said: 'Just remember that no-one will ever do the job the way you would have done it. But that doesn't mean that they won't do it just as well.'

He had a point. I cringed occasionally at the odd letter that went out but at least it went out and didn't sit on my floor for weeks. We had a partner at Levingtons that wouldn't trust anyone to do his work. One day a client stormed in and had him pinned up against the wall because he hadn't done a mortgage reference that he'd promised to do weeks before and the client had lost out on the chance to buy his dream home. The juniors did laugh about it although I don't think the partner, or the client was laughing much. He was one of those that thought that Ron Mortimore was a bit unprofessional but at least Ron's clients knew he was on their side."

Ruby pondered what she'd heard. It actually sounded a bit more interesting that she'd expected but somehow she got the impression that whilst Matt admired the slightly chaotic way Ron Mortimore had run his business, he was a little more organised himself.

Chapter 5

Are you a Ronald or an Elton?

The day-to-day reality for most people running small businesses is that they spend more of their time working in the business rather than on the business.

When you started your business, the service you provided was excellent. You had enough hours in the day to ensure all customers were dealt with personally. You built up a good reputation with your clients. Your work was to a high standard. As a result, you kept getting new customers, so you took on new staff. Your bookkeeper or accountant looked after the payroll and made it sound as if that was all you needed to worry about.

But ever since you took on staff, things have not been as good.

Service standards have slipped. You're now spending a lot more time doing admin and when you're not doing admin it feels like you're spending your time putting right things that your new staff have got wrong. Customers don't seem as happy anymore and you feel like your hard-earned reputation is slipping.

Chapter 5

The solution is often to start working on your business not in it - to put together systems, identify roles, recruit and train.

Or is it? What if you are actually at a crossroads with more than one direction that you can go? The first thing to consider is whether you want to be a Ronald or an Elton.

Ok bear with me on this. I do know the history of the McDonalds brothers, Ray Kroc etc. But let's imagine that it was really Ronald who started the whole thing. After years of flipping burgers and entertaining the kids, Ronald has now stepped back from the front line and trained up others to wear the flipper-like shoes and red nose.

Ensconced at the top of McDonalds tower in a smart designer suit, with his bright red hair receding a bit and carrying a heavy hint of grey, he works on strategy, marketing, recruitment and systems. He's built a franchise that can be replicated all over the world.

Where once he did everything, now his influence goes unseen. In the background, tweaking, working with his Board to build their skills with shares and options worth millions.

Ok, back to reality.

On a smaller and more realistic scale, Ronald the owner-manager has realised that the mini-me he's been looking for, doesn't exist. But by putting in the hours and applying real attention to detail on the internal systems of his business, he's also managed to step back from the front line.

The business no longer depends on him.

Holidays are more frequent. And now that it's no longer dependent on him, the business is now much more sellable. A potential buyer (a much bigger company from a connected industry who wants to get into a new market) has been sniffing around. A lucrative sale followed by either a comfortable retirement or new challenges beckons.

Chapter 5

It's an image that appeals to many business owners. Usually, the ones who have enough money in the bank but not enough time to enjoy it.

Or maybe those who just feel stressed or anxious about their day to day lives.

The appeal of working on their business and not in it, is strong. They want to be a Ronald.

A small percentage of those who head off on that journey make it. Many are pulled back in far too easily by the smallest problem.

In the Godfather III, Michael Corleone thinks that he has finally met the promise to his wife (two movies earlier) to escape criminality. His attempts to set up a legitimate business are sabotaged by his underworld contacts though.

"Just when I thought I was out, they pull me back in," he says just before his heart attack.

Ever felt like that?

Of course you have, if the business is too dependent on you.

But sometimes the 'they' is not a 'they' but a 'you'.

It's difficult to admit that a significant portion your business's success is very much driven by your personality and skills.

And that's not the end of the world. As long as your business model accepts that.

Before you head down the path to Ronald-dom (is that a word? it is now), ask yourself what you want. Do you have the skills to make the changes to your business to make your business completely independent of you? Are you prepared to invest the time and money required to make those changes?

Chapter 5

Does that approach even work in your industry? Has anyone else made it work?

Because Ronalds aren't the only financial success stories out there.

Take Elton John - he's one of the most financially successful people in the UK. The one thing he hasn't done is train up lots of little Elton Johns to go round the country performing Goodbye Yellow Brick Road every Saturday night.

That's because he's the star performer. He's the one they want.

Is that like you? Are you the star performer? Are you the one who earns the money that the business earns? Would the business be able to operate without your talents?

If so, then you're an Elton and that means you need a business model which is very different to those of a Ronald.

The key for Eltons is to rid themselves of the tasks that someone else can do. Get a PA, a good accountant, bookkeeper and all-round marketing specialist. Download a really good dictation app so you can dictate letters and instructions. Delegate everything apart from the things that no-one else but you can do.

Use the skills and expertise you have, to deliver a quality which is better than your competitors and then make sure you charge for your services accordingly. There's only one of you, so you better be focussed on earning as much as you can for each day that you work.

Some 'Eltons' forget the last bit but it's crucial because when you can no longer do what you do, there will be no business to sell. Because the business is you! Unless you are the real Elton John and are likely to be receiving royalties, you're going to have to squirrel away enough of what you earn to build an investment fund that you can live off when you retire.

Chapter 5

And if that works for you, then that's great. You've probably bought the wrong book though because this book is for aspiring Ronalds.

Or maybe those who want to be a bit more Ronald than they currently are. And a little bit less Elton!

The reality is that very few people are 100% Ronald or 100% Elton. Most of us are a little bit of both. We just realise that we can't be as Elton as we have been before because there's the risk that we might burn out, or not earn enough to invest enough to have enough to retire on.

So we better carry on making the business less dependent on you.

Chapter 6

Pause for thought

Whilst Ben's morning was providing plenty of food for thought, so was David's.

'The funeral of Peter Arthur Leonard Lamb' read David looking at the familiar face of his old friend and associate on the order of service.

As he entered the small chapel in Wickfield Crematorium, the front row seemed to be split along family lines. On the left were Peter's first family; his ex-wife Barbara, their two grown up children Adam and Becky plus Peter's elderly Mum. On the right-hand pew, Peter's second wife Toni and the son from her first marriage, Elliott.

David had always liked Barbara and David's wife Jean got on really well with her. He'd never quite warmed to Toni though and Jean had always thought that Bright Interiors should have found themselves another courier company when Peter left Barbara for Toni three years earlier.

But there were always two sides to every story, and he trusted Peter, so he kept doing business with him.

Chapter 6

Then Toni got involved in the business and for a while it looked like she improved things. Peter was a loveable rogue in truth but not the best at paperwork, but Toni got him a bit more organised. David had found that Toni wasn't quite as flexible on credit terms as Peter had been but initially admired her for getting a little bit tougher. He was a little bit more irritated when the boot was on the other foot though and Toni took four months to pay a bill from Bright's. "One rule for them and another for everyone else" was David's analysis at the time.

Jean had forbidden him from inviting Peter and Toni to their traditional New Year's Eve party as well which he had reluctantly agreed to. It had all made it slightly awkward for him the first time he saw Peter every New Year when they had the obligatory conversation about the Christmas and New Year break both knowing about the party and both knowing Peter and his second wife had not been invited. This year's traditional awkward conversation had taken place only three weeks earlier, the last time David saw Peter alive.

One by one the other mourners entered, their unspoken loyalty guiding them towards the left-hand side of the chapel rather than the right until the left-hand side was virtually full whilst the right hand side contained only Toni's family, those who were unaware of the politics of the situation and twelve burly men who represented the workforce of Awesome Haulage.

Once upon a time David would have known all their names but now he knew only a few. Only two remained since Toni had joined the firm and those were the moaners who complained about everything from the colour of the livery on their vans to the performance of their local football team and the Prime Minister. 'Mood hoovers' thought David; "they suck the energy and joy from a room when they walk into it".

"Shove up young man," said a voice right next to him. Trevor! His oldest employee. Well employee wasn't quite the right word since Trevor had retired eleven years ago. "I don't want to stop the young 'uns getting their chance at this place so I'm going to retire now," he'd told David about a month before his 65th birthday "but if you ever need me to help

Chapter 6

out on anything at all, just give me a ring. I won't be available in December though because I'm going to be Father Christmas at the local shopping centre and I won't cancel any of my bowls matches for work but other than that, it's up to you."

For a few months, David hadn't rung him but then they got busy, and he made the call. Trevor was there at 7.30am the following morning loading stud partitioning onto a van as if he'd never been away. In the end, Trevor worked more days for Bright's than he had off, except in December of course. At 76, Trevor was as energetic and enthusiastic as anyone David had working for him and because he didn't actually need the work, he was unafraid to tell David his opinion. "You've got to have a word with your eldest" Trevor told David one day. "He's bloody good at his work, but he can't manage people for toffee. If it wasn't for Phil Morrison, you'd have no-one working there, the way Joe goes on."

Apart from the fact that he was twenty years older than him, David envied Trevor a little. He seemed to do so much with his life; bowls club, tennis, swimming plus he was always taking one or more of his nine grandchildren somewhere or other. Last Summer Trevor even told David that he'd been go-karting with one of his grandchildren. Go-karting! At 76! "Never get stuck in a rut young man." was what Trevor told David. "The only difference between a rut and a grave is the depth." How true.

Soon the whole chapel was full, even the right-hand side, and it was then standing room only. Good turnout for the loveable old rogue thought David.

David's mind drifted to some of the other funerals of business acquaintances he'd been to. They were all the same. Always dead before they'd ever had the time to enjoy the trappings of the wealth their businesses had created.

Halfway through the service, a mutual friend called Stelios stood up to give a little speech about how he'd first met Peter and told a story about some of the stunts they had pulled when they were first in business.

Chapter 6

Everyone loved Stelios; he was the sort of guy who would do anything for anyone and expect them to do nothing in return.

"If you want something doing right, you've got to do it yourself." he'd told David years earlier. But the years seemed to be catching up with Stelios now. The bulbous nose and red cheeks were a giveaway that he was using alcohol to smooth over the difficult edges of his life and David had heard a rumour that Stelios's building business was in trouble financially. He'd better be careful, thought David "otherwise the next funeral will be his". It crossed his mind that perhaps it might be his own, but he banished the thought quickly.

Outside the crematorium, there was still family tension in the air and David decided he'd make his escape before finding himself forced to declare his allegiance. He found a moment to speak to Barbara, mumbled something about being "snowed under at work" and headed for the sanctuary of his Tesla managing to avoid any eye contact with Elliott as he left. Elliott was worse than Toni. Working there as 'commercial manager' or some kind of nonsense title that had been dreamed up to create a job for him, his impact seemed to be to generally irritate customers, suppliers and employees to a similar degree without advancing the company one iota.

Once inside his vehicle, he looked at the mobile which had been on silent during the funeral. There was a text message from Phil Morrison. "What time are you coming back? I really need to talk to you about something." 'Oh god, what now?' wondered David.

Section B
Taking control

Chapter 7

Silver spoon or balls of steel

I'm sure you will be familiar with the traditional learning curve. You know the one where it goes up quite rapidly at the start and then slowly starts to plateau out. In theory, everybody continually improves but after a while the rate of improvement is so marginal that it's barely noticeable.

In practice it doesn't actually work like that though.

One of my closest friends worked for one of the major banks and they assessed the performance of all their financial advisers. What they found was that after two years the performance of those financial advisers peaked. Then it dropped for a while and then having dropped a bit it then bottomed out. It then remained at a flat level pretty much for the rest of their careers.

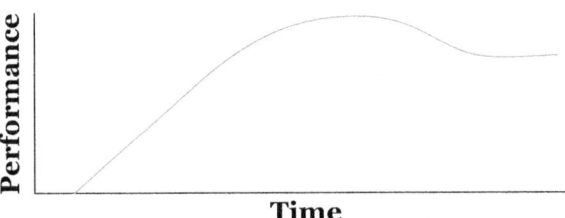

Chapter 7

What happened was that when you are going up the learning curve at the start it's exciting. Everything is interesting, and you're engaged with what you do. But when the work starts to repeat itself, you can get a little bit bored, and your performance will drop.

But of course, by then you know what you are doing and are actually quite good at whatever you do so your performance only drops so far, before it plateaus out. Welcome to the rut!

All businesses (and business owners) will find themselves in that sort of rut every now and again. The first one is often about 5 or 10 years into their journey. This is when your management style is evolving, and you are building your skills. Eventually you get to that point where without some big changes, you are always going to be where you currently are.

And what then?

Well, you can keep tweaking and fine-tuning and take on some Elton-like characteristics. Maybe you can find yourself a side hustle that is more of an investment than a business (usually with property of some kind). Be careful though, sometimes side hustles can take up so much of your time and energy that they affect the main part of the business.

Or you can take a chance and make a change.

This is where you need to be brave because it might not work out. You might find yourself licking your wounds two years down the line having put a huge amount of time and / or money into whatever it is that you tried to do.

Of course, this is what being an entrepreneur is all about. Taking a risk.

The first question you need to consider is how much of a risk are you prepared to take?

Are you prepared to risk everything you have for the chance of building a multi-million pound firm?

Chapter 7

There are usually two types of people who will do that:
- Those with very rich parents who will bail them out in the event of disaster
- Those with balls of steel

If you don't fit either of those categories, then you have a balancing act to do. Because there are only factors that you are chasing at this stage:

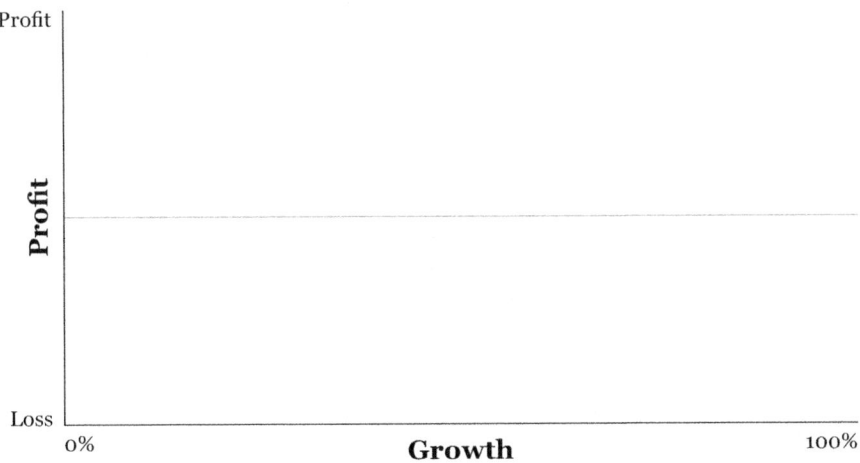

Of course, the two have an implicit relationship. Manage your growth in the right way and it will convert into good profits. Re-invest those profits into marketing, technology, training and all those other things that drive growth and further growth will come.

There are two key metrics here:
- Percentage rate of growth
- Net profit as a percentage of turnover

Chapter 7

There is a trade-off between these two metrics which is based on your attitude to risk. This is shown on the three graphs below.

Someone with a high attitude to risk and a high desire to grow would have a graph that looks something like this:

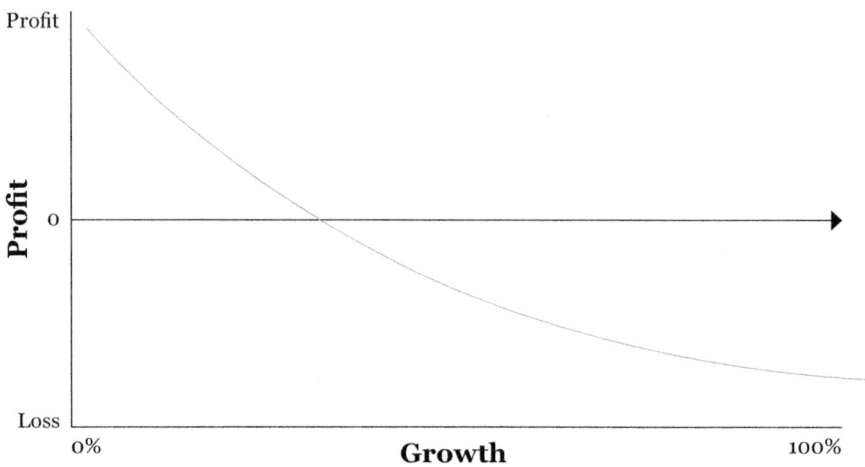

As you can see, someone with that mindset would be prepared to suffer losses in order to achieve high levels of growth. This is of course the path that many dot com businesses of the early part of this century followed. Amazon for example had 8 years of losses before achieving a profit.

Many of those businesses never made it to profit of course and no longer exist.

For smaller owner-managed businesses, the risk is not that they never make it into profit but that they can't finance their growth. Or even if they can, the management team can't handle all the challenges growth brings and mistakes start to happen.

On the other hand, someone with a low attitude to risk and a higher desire for profit than growth would have a graph that looks something like this:

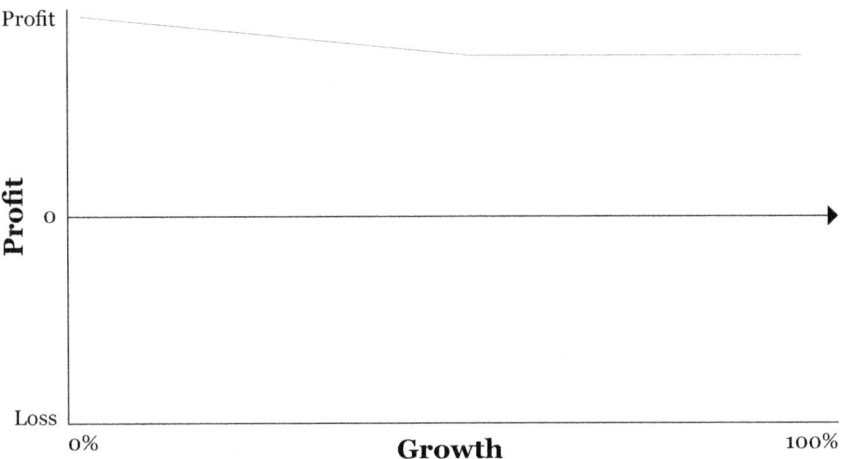

High desire for profit

One of my clients once called me on a Monday to tell me about an article he had read in a Sunday newspaper business section that said that no good business should be functioning without an overdraft. He asked me what he was doing wrong. He was very profitable.

The answer was that he was 'under-trading'. In business terms, he should have been maximising the potential of his business by borrowing and expanding.

But he didn't want to do that. He was happy. He had more than enough money to keep him happy. Good for him.

For most of us there is a gentler trade-off between growth and profit and our graph would look something like this.

Chapter 7

The line on your graph will be different to mine and to everyone else's.

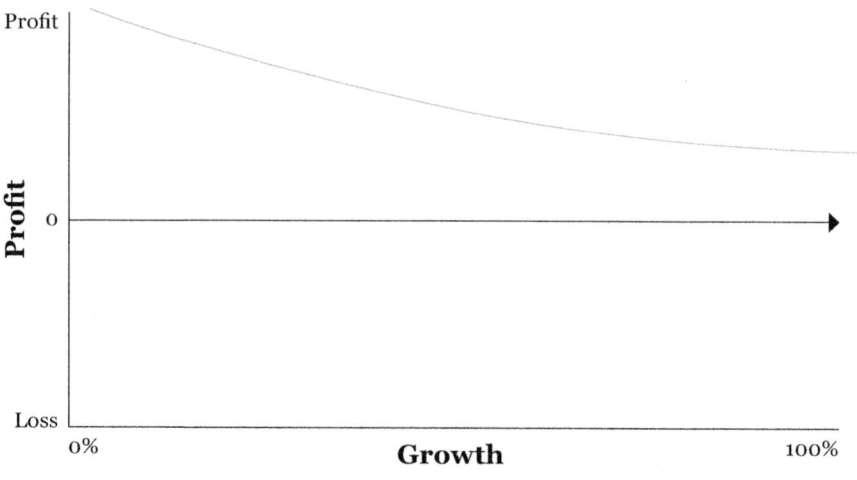

Gentle trade off

You just have to decide where it is.

Everyone's definition of success is different. If you weren't born with a silver spoon in your mouth, you don't necessarily need balls of steel, but they might need to be made of aluminium at least.

Chapter 8

If only they all had the same attitude as Phil

Back in Ruby's world, it had been an interesting first day. She was starting to get a good feel for the culture of the firm she'd just joined and had learnt something for free that it might take some of her peers many years to learn.

This guy Mortimore that Matt was talking about, seemed a bit more fearless than the likes of Uncle Eric. He wasn't afraid to delegate. He didn't seem to have spent his whole life worrying about whether people were mucking things up. She got the feeling though that there was more to Matt Pevy than a carbon copy of his old boss though and was interested to learn more.

She pondered what she had learnt whilst driving home. Maybe that people given more responsibility make fewer mistakes than those without responsibility.

She resolved to talk to Dad over dinner that evening, little knowing the day that he had just experienced.

Chapter 8

After all, the benefits of effective delegation were well documented in some of the business books she'd read since finishing her degree. They just seemed to be all theory though and now she was seeing the theory being put into practice.

But how could she bring this up with him? Maybe 'Dad, do you think that delegation is more about sharing responsibility for tasks with others or do you think it is more about abdicating responsibility?' Perhaps that might work if she was a hostile TV interviewer and Dad some junior government minister but not if she didn't want to get thrown out before she'd saved up enough for a flat of her own! She needed to be more subtle or say nothing at all.

But she wasn't about to say nothing. After all, the one thing she was pretty sure of was that Dad needed to make some changes and needed to stop trying to do everything himself.

Delegation would allow him to assign and coordinate tasks and resources more effectively and free him up to do the stuff that no-one else at Bright Interiors could do rather than spending his time doing work that others could do or putting right the things that they had messed up.

She was starting to see things from the employees' point of view as well.

Better delegation would help them develop their skills and knowledge and enable them to assume greater responsibility. Plus, it would make their work a bit more interesting with some tasks offering a challenge and opportunity to shine.

Surely if Dad could delegate in the correct way, he'd be under less pressure and some of his staff might be able to come up with some improvements to the way they do things. Matt believed that the faster a company can come to a decision the more efficient it became. And more accurate decision-making results in better customer service and greater competitiveness.

Chapter 8

For the first time in her life, she felt quite excited about something she'd learnt at work and had already worked out how he was going to get it into the conversation over dinner.

As she drove up the road towards the house, her hopes were boosted by the sight of her father's Tesla on the drive then dashed by the sight of two green vans with familiar number plates. Her two brothers were home as well which only meant one thing. Crisis!

Whilst there was plenty of space to talk about things at work, when there was something really big happening, they always came back home to keep the crisis away from the employees. This didn't work of course as it was actually a recipe for allowing rumour and uncertainty to build up back at the firm.

As she quietly entered the living room, her eldest brother Joe was in full flow. "He's an idiot Dad. He lets the staff run rings round him and we pay him too much money. You're well rid of him."

"Who?" asked Ruby innocently.

"Phil." answered his other brother Daniel. "Phil Morrison has gone off and joined up with James and Marcus. They're all plotting against us to steal our business."

"He hasn't joined James and Marcus", insisted David. "He said he's going to work for a recruitment company."

"Phil's gone to work for a recruitment company? Why would he do that?" asked Ruby.

"Because it's not true" screamed Joe warming to his theme. "He's joined those deceitful back-stabbing morons who left us three months ago. It's obvious."

It didn't make sense to Ruby. She had got to know Phil really well in the few months that he had worked at the firm, and she knew that Phil was

Chapter 8

as loyal to the firm as anyone who had ever worked there. It had been his first job at 16 and fifteen years later he'd become integral to the firm. It was almost as if he'd become the fourth brother although Joe who had always been slightly jealous of Phil, would never have agreed.

"Well I don't believe it," said Jean entering the room as she handed out plates of chicken pie and mash to her husband and children, having concluded that the only way they were going to eat tonight was if she put the plates in their hands or on their laps. "If he's left, he's got his reasons, and it won't be to join Stanmore Butler that's for sure."

"When is he leaving?" asked Ruby. "He's gone." Dad replied. "I told him if he could do this to us now, he might as well go straight away."

An awkward hush descended on the room as they attacked their dinners and avoided conversation.

"Well at least one of us has had a good day." said Ruby finally breaking the silence.

"Really? Tell us all about it." said her mother grateful for a change of subject.

Ruby started to tell her audience about how excited she was by her new job. "The way things are organised it looks like I'll get to do loads of different stuff in my first six months. Not like the six months adding up columns of figures that Uncle Eric said he used to do when he was a trainee."

Ruby thought it might be a good idea to talk about Matt hoping that his father might see that there was a different way.

She had a theory about why her father found it so hard to delegate. Her father was a perfectionist and was basically frightened that other people would not do the job to his same high standards. But they never were going to meet those same high standards on their own. They might do with training and opportunity, but they were getting neither. As a

Chapter 8

result, they then lacked the skills to do the more complicated aspects of their work all of which convinced David Bright that he couldn't trust them. It had become a vicious circle.

There was one exception of course. Phil Morrison.

He'd set himself high standards and had always sought responsibility rather than waiting fruitlessly like his colleagues. For whatever reason, Phil saw himself as part of the family and took it on his himself to find the best way to do everything and did everything to the highest standard possible.

He even challenged David over stuff that he was about to do. "That potential customer in Woolwich. Why can't I go and see them?" Eventually David would relent, and he'd let Phil get on with it. He rarely regretted it. 'If only they all had the same attitude as Phil' was something the brothers heard their father say many times over the years. Ruby could see why his father felt so let down by Phil's sudden resignation.

"Matt says that most business owners are too frightened of what can go wrong to trust their staff, but Matt gives everyone a list of the roles that they are responsible for and the tasks that each role is responsible for undertaking so that everyone knows what they should be doing."

There was an uncomfortable pause as Ruby waited for her wise words to hit their mark and everyone else waited long enough to change the subject without appearing rude.

"Who's going to keep the London customers sweet then, Dad?" said Daniel the quietest of the three siblings who secretly appreciated the skills that Phil brought to the family firm.

"Well, I suppose I'll have to." said David, resignation in his voice that neither of his sons were capable for different reasons of looking after a portfolio of hi-tech professional firms who paid Bright Interiors a lot of money to look after their needs. Another silence followed whilst the enormity of David's workload sunk in.

Chapter 8

As they all thought slightly different thoughts, Ruby's returned to something that Matt had said to him. "People who say they can't delegate because they can't get the staff might be really unlucky but more often than not it's their own fault for either not recruiting well, not hanging on to the good staff they have got, not training them properly or perhaps it's simply a case that they can delegate but are just too frightened to. The biggest mistake most business owners make is upward delegation where they allow one of their team to pass a problem back onto them rather than give that employee the help they need, to solve the problem."

"You should read 'The one-minute manager meets the monkey'." Suggested Ruby, breaking the silence. "The what?" said David.

"It's a really good business book. Matt mentioned it to me today. I think you should read it."

"I don't have time for books," said David. "There's simply too much to do." But a more subtler point had been made in the room, one that Jean and Daniel had picked up on.

"I think you should go and have a chat with Matt" said Jean. "I think you need to get a clear perspective on things, and I think he'll provide that. You always said you wished you could get your business as well organised as his was."

David shuffled uneasily in his favourite armchair.

"For goodness sake, that's why you helped Ruby get the job there. So, she didn't have to put up with all the problems and stress you've had to deal with all these years."

Jean didn't make many of the decisions in the house or state her opinion that often but when she did, they all knew she was right.

Chapter 9

What next?

I once listened to a really good business speaker speak to an entire room of business owners and say to them that he was going to tell them how they could get four holidays per year.

There was a really long pause. Everyone leaned in.

Then he said, "go to the travel agent and book them." So far so obvious!

Of course, what he was really saying was that if we don't get those things booked into the diary then they are never going to happen. Because there will always be something else to do.

Ok, I know what you're thinking. The week before the last big holiday you had was so stressful that you spent the first half of the holiday coming down from the adrenaline high and the second half of the holiday worrying about all the things you needed to do when you got back. And let's not even get started on the week after you got back.

But if it's your business, it's easy for work to push everything else out and take over. It's even easier to fall back on the skills that got you here in the

Chapter 9

first place and just do it yourself. First, you start getting in earlier in the morning, then you start leaving late at night, then it's Saturday morning. On and on it goes.

Of course, somewhere along the line, you build some really good juggling skills.

It is great when you have an organised to do list that you can work your way down methodically all day. But of course, some days you just get loads of emails, phone calls, questions and you must make decisions about what you are going to deal with next.

This is all the sort of stuff that is covered on the time management training that I know many of you have had. But let's have a little re-cap anyway.

Is it important? Is it urgent?

How much time do you spend in each of the four quadrants i.e.:
1. Urgent and important
2. Important not urgent
3. Urgent not important
4. Not urgent not important

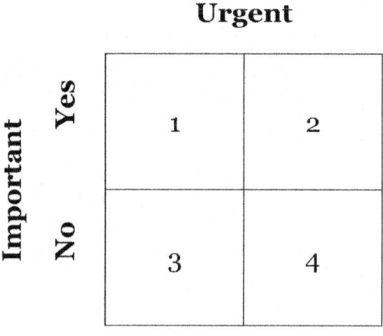

Chapter 9

The average person's time is split roughly as follows:
1. Urgent and important   30%
2. Important not urgent   10%
3. Urgent not important   50%
4. Not urgent not important   10%

Urgent

	Yes	No
Important Yes	30%	10%
Important No	50%	10%

The elephant in the room of course is why we would spend 10% of our time on things which are not urgent and not important? Because we secretly enjoy them perhaps?

But that's not the biggest difference between the average person and high achievers, whose time is more like:
- Urgent and important   10%
- Important not urgent   60%
- Urgent not important   30%
- Not urgent not important   0%

Urgent

	Yes	No
Important Yes	10%	60%
Important No	30%	0%

Chapter 9

The basic premise is that because high achievers spend more time on things that are important but not urgent (usually activities that make the business run more efficiently), then as a result less urgent stuff crops up.

That's the theory though. In the real world, you must make real decisions and each of us have brains which have been trained to think in a particular way.

It may be that in your work life, the roles that you undertake are primarily focused around deadlines.

As you get better at your role you start to work backwards from those deadlines.

You start to get a good inkling when the volume of work is higher than it should be at a particular time of the month or year. You know how to react to those situations. You know when a project must be started by. You know when it's in danger of falling behind.

Then you take on some other responsibilities - ones which are not deadline driven. In fact, they are simply based on the profitability of your business or maybe the growth. Classic important but not urgent tasks. The bad news is that you will probably never get around to doing them if your thought process is all based on deadlines.

Besides there are far too many important not urgent tasks that you can do which could fill up your day three or four times over.

You can't do them all, so if you've got lots of urgent not important tasks under your nose, you just get on and do those and then a day goes by and a week and a month and a year later something that was really important but not at all urgent has not been done.

The implications of that might be that you have had to do lots more work on a particular task because the system change that you needed to make or the training that you needed to undertake or the staffing issue that you needed to resolve never did get sorted then as a consequence you ended

Chapter 9

up with far more work to do than you would have done otherwise.

It is easy to be wise in hindsight. But how can you be wise in foresight?

To do so requires an understanding of return on investment (ROI).

ROI is a term which is used by people that are buying businesses, or properties or just by business analysts generally. It is asking you to work out return divided by cost as a percentage. 15% might be a good ROI for somebody who is an investor in businesses. It's a lot better than they would get from a savings or general investment account.

In your world, there might be something which is a 1000% ROI. There might be something which you could spend an hour on now which would save you 10 hours in the future. That is a 1,000% return.

When you are faced with a long list of things that you could do which are important but not urgent, it is crucial that you consider their ROI. Then you can compare them to some of the other urgent but not important things as well and prioritise based on which ROI is the highest.

Let me give you an example.

Let's say you have two queries to deal with from customers. Ideally, you should deal with both today. You have also got a member of your team who needs an hour of your time in order to be able to do their work for the rest of their week. You have three things to do, and you only have enough time for two of them. Which do you do?

Well, I can't answer that, because I don't know what your return is on any of those things, and I don't know what your alternatives are.

Let's say one of the queries is for a fee for £5,000 and the other is a fee for £50. That would probably mean that the £5,000 one would trump the £50 one every day of the week.

Or maybe not. It may be that the £5,000 one is for a customer who is

Chapter 9

actually quite busy this week and it won't do any harm to deal with it next week. And the £50 one is for a long-term customer who has been really upset by a particularly trivial item, especially after some mistakes have been made on their work recently.

Suddenly the return on the £50 job is actually bigger than on the £5,000 job.

But what about a member of staff that needed some guidance from you?

You may be thinking that the return is avoiding the loss that the company is going to suffer if that person sits around twiddling their thumbs for the rest of the week. And you'd be right although you might not be the only person who can solve that problem. Perhaps there is another solution.

Perhaps you could ask one of your colleagues if they could undertake the training.

They might not do quite as well as you because they might not have quite the same amount of knowledge. The difference in performance of the member of staff receiving the training may be quite small though. Therefore the return on your time for doing that training is the difference between that person's performance if you do the training or that person's performance if one of your colleagues does the training.

Suddenly the return isn't quite so big (when compared to the best alternative), is it?

I could give you a million examples of when you have got to compare one project against another but of course you don't have the time to sit down and analyse all this out on a great big spreadsheet. You must have your 'to do list' in front of you and make a judgement.

Just like anything else, if you practice this stuff, you get better at it and eventually your instincts take over. After 30 years running my accountancy practice, I think I am pretty good judge of what would get the best return on the next hour of my time.

Chapter 9

So, whenever you get a visit from that horrible feeling of overwhelm, there is only thing to do. Go to your to do list, delete all the numbers down the side, make sure everything that you are going to do is on that to do list and then put it back into a new order based on return on investment.

And if the thing at the top is not screaming at you to be the thing to do next, think about booking that holiday.

Chapter 10

It's all about "levewage"

Ruby set the alarm to get up early and was in the office by 8, almost bumping into Matt as he unlocked. "Blimey, you're keen" he said. "Yes" said Ruby "but that's not why I'm here so early. I wanted to have a chat with you about Dad's business".

"OK" said Matt as they walked through reception. "Problems?"

Ruby started talking through the events of the previous day before they had even had a chance to sit down, and Matt mentally took it all in. He had warned David before about the risk he was taking with Marcus and James, but he was shocked to hear that Phil was leaving as well. Once Ruby had talked everything through, Matt told him what the next step should be.

"Before he makes any rash decisions about the future of the company, we need to have a strategic planning session. I normally recommend a whole day, but I've got no chance of convincing your Dad on that one." said Matt. "Give him a ring and see if he's available this afternoon for a couple of hours. I think Joe and Daniel ought to come as well. If we don't get their commitment to any changes, then the whole thing is doomed to fail."

Chapter 10

Ruby messaged the family WhatsApp group suggesting an appointment with Matt and agreement was swiftly reached for a 1 o'clock meeting.

"Matt, can I ask you something?" said Ruby. "I've seen the way that you operate around here, and I really think that Dad's business needs to take on board some of the things that you do. But I wondered why you'd never advised Dad to do some of those things."

"Oh, believe me I've tried!" said Matt. "But your Dad's been running his business for a long time and I guess he's comfortable doing things his way. I've brought a few things up in meetings in the past couple of years, but I get the feeling that if I pushed any harder, I'd end up upsetting him and losing a client, which isn't particularly good for business!"

"I guess he is a bit stubborn." replied Ruby sheepishly.

After getting a coffee, Ruby asked Matt why he was doing the training rather than anyone else.

"Well, it's not actually one of my roles but I do deputize. Lisa normally does inductions as part of her role as training manager but she's off doing some exams at the moment. We're planning some significant growth this year though, and I want to get the induction systems absolutely spot on and this seemed to be the best way. Besides, I thought I'd find out what your Dad says about me behind my back!"

"Dad's always quite complimentary about you. He thought you looked a bit young when you first took over, but he decided not to hold that against you!"

"Mmm, it was an interesting first year. I thought I knew it all when I first took over, but there was a lot more to running a business than I'd realised. I'd been with Ron Mortimore for about three years, and it was quite a learning curve but good fun."

"Is Ron Mortimore still around?"

Chapter 10

"Yeah, I see him from time to time. He had a heart attack about two weeks after I took over this place. I think he just stretched himself a bit too far."

"All those meetings he kept forgetting?"

"Not just that. A lot of things revolved around him, although Chas and I took a lot of responsibility. It was a laugh though. Chas was always a good crack to work with. He was a year younger than me but one of those guys who passes every exam at the first attempt and really sharp. We always bounced ideas off each other and Ron was always coming up with new ideas as well. You see that trophy over there?"

Ruby looked over to the bookcase and saw the strangest looking cup she'd ever seen. It was about three inches high and twelve inches wide.

"Funny looking cup." she commented.

"There's a story about that cup. Ron couldn't pronounce his Rs so he suggested we play for the Wyder Cup. And if it was going to be the Wyder Cup, it needed a wider cup! He got it specially made."

"And you won it?"

"Only once actually. We played about six times. The first three included Ron but he had to give up golf after the heart attack. Chas and I played a few more times but he just got too busy. Last time was about 5 years ago."

"Do you still speak to Chas?"

"Not anymore, although I hear things through the grapevine occasionally. He's doing ok, but I don't think he's Mr Popular with the staff. He can get pretty snappy when he's under pressure and a few people have taken exception to that and just upped sticks and left."

"Why do you think he's like that?"

Chapter 10

"Well, Chas just picked up from where Ron left off. We'd just done this deal to buy Eric's business here, so I'd come up to Wickfield and they were looking for a replacement then Ron had his heart attack. Chas was a Trojan at the time. He just rolled up his sleeves and got on with doing not just his job but Ron's as well. The other staff all pulled together of course, and the clients were quite understanding but he still had this huge personal workload and it's like he just never caught up."

"So he really struggled?"

"In terms of time available yes, but financially he did really well. Ron took the heart attack as a wakeup call and asked Chas and me if we would buy him out. It just made more sense for me to buy this office and Chas to buy the main practice in Compton. Compton was a much bigger practice of course so Chas had to borrow a lot more than me, but Ron was pretty helpful by agreeing that we could pay some of his money in instalments."

"Well Dad always tells this joke about Father Christmas, a poor accountant and a rich accountant in a lift. Which one presses the button? The rich accountant of course because the other two don't exist!"

"Oh, if I had a pound for every time that I've heard that one! He's got a point; most of us are in demand and always able to earn a good living. Not many practices are that profitable though."

"But you said they all make a good living."

"They do. But a lot of professionals whether they're accountants, solicitors or whatever only really make the same or a bit more than they would earn if they got a job. They don't achieve leverage."

"Leverage?"

"Yeah by leverage, I mean how you leverage your time. Essentially, it's the ratio between the number of owners and the number of staff. The more staff per owner then the more profitable it should be for the owner. In most small practices, the amount of time that the owner would charge

Chapter 10

is pretty similar. Add to that the profit on each member of staff and take off the overheads and that's what the owner actually earns. The more staff you have, the more profit you make as long as everyone has plenty of work to do."

"But Chas had good leverage?"

"We all did really. Ron was always going on about leverage or 'levewage' as he called it!"

Ruby paused to think about Dad's business and whether leverage applied to him, but Matt had other plans.

"Come on, young Ruby, we've still got a training programme to get through."

About ten minutes after the training session had ended, Ruby saw her father's Tesla pulling up in the car park outside and her father and two brothers getting out. She got the feeling that Matt might have a slightly harder time convincing Joe of his ideas. When she was confident that the three of them and Matt were safely ensconced in the firm's boardroom, she slipped outside to make a quick phone call on her mobile.

"Phil? It's Ruby. Ruby Bright. Yeah, I know; Dad told me." There was an uncomfortable silence for a few seconds. "Listen Phil, do you think we could meet for a chat at lunchtime? I just want to find out what happened." With lunchtime arrangements made, Ruby returned to her desk.

Back in the boardroom, Matt had a familiar approach to strategic planning sessions. If there was more than one person from a particular business, Matt always asked his first question to the least opinionated of those present and then worked his way up. He started with Daniel.

"Daniel, I just want you to imagine yourself three years in the future. The business is exactly the way you would like it to be. Describe it to me. What does it look like? What is it like for you to work in it?"

Chapter 10

Slightly thrown by being asked to give his answer first, and with his opinion not affected by anyone else's having gone before, Daniel answered honestly although his answers seem to focus entirely on the financial benefits that his ideal version would bring and very little on the day-to-day details required to achieve financial success.

Matt turned to Joe and asked the same question. Joe saw running the business as his birthright, so the question elicited far more information. As is fairly typical in those situations, Joe focussed on the present rather than the future.

"Our biggest problem are our staff. There is hardly anyone that I'd keep on. They don't use their initiative and are out the door the second the clock hits five. I'm always having to correct their mistakes. They just don't really care and are more interested in gambling on their phones than doing a good job."

Satisfied that he'd summed up the situation perfectly, Joe sat back to allow the unpalatable truth to be digested by everyone else in the room.

"They're not all like that." said Dan. Joe wasn't used to being contradicted by his little brother. His smart-arse younger sister maybe, but not Dan.

"Trevor isn't like that, and neither was Phil." corrected Dan.

"But Trevor is technically retired, and Phil doesn't work for us anymore, which is why I think we're all here, isn't it?" said Joe.

"And some of the others wouldn't be like it if you weren't quite so rude to them." said the newly emboldened Dan.

"Is it my turn?" interjected David suddenly aware of the early stages of a potentially damaging dispute. "I think it's too simple to say that we don't have good staff. I think that we might have better staff than we realise but they just aren't motivated."

Chapter 10

"Why do you think that is?" said Matt aware that his presence was starting to allow the family to get a few things off their chest perhaps for the first time in years.

David continued. *"Well I guess it's because I don't motivate them well enough. Maybe I should be spending a bit more time doing staff reviews and stuff like that."*

"Can I mention something?" asked Matt. *"Neither you nor Joe have answered the question and told me where you want to be in three years' time. You've just focussed on the present difficulties. Joe, how would you like things to be in three years' time?"*

"OK. Well I'd like me and Dan to be running the business and Dad enjoying his retirement, playing a lot of golf, taking Mum to places they've never had time to go to." Joe's body language showed that he thought that was a good answer.

"David?" queried Matt feeling perhaps he knew his client better than his sons did.

"Well I don't see myself being retired, that's for certain. I enjoy my work especially when we do a good job. I like most of the customers and even some of the staff are good fun to work with. I'd like a bit more time at home but if I wasn't working at all, we'd get under each other's feet, and I think I'd drive your mother mad." he nodded at Joe and Dan who agreed that was probably what would happen.

"I'd just like a bit more 'me' time. What you said I should be doing Joe – you're right. But I could do all those things if I had a day or two off a week and a few more weeks' holiday."

"So what's stopping you from doing that now?" asked Matt.

David raised his eyebrows and puffed. *"Sorry boys, but I'm going to be honest here. There are 18 maybe 19 mortgages and food bills depending on me. If I did less hours, there would be more cock-ups with orders, cash*

Chapter 10

flow would be all over the place because half the customers would drag their feet over paying us even more than they do now, you two would be arguing most of the time, half the staff would be in tears over the way that Joe talks to them and I'd end up not enjoying a single moment of my time off because I'd be spending all my time worrying about what was going on back in the business." David paused. "Basically, the place is too dependent on me!"

Matt broke the silence aware that for the first time in his life the Bright family patriarch and provider had shown weakness and expressed to his sons how he really felt.

"Have you ever come across the outcome, performance, process approach to achieving what you want from your business?"

Chapter 11

Set the hares running

Once you've got your to do list put in an order based on ROI, the tempting thing to do at this point would be to just get going on the top thing on the list. That would probably be a mistake though.

The first thing you need to do is to set some hares running. Before I explain, let's go back to how you got where you are today.

In terms of your workload, you will have busier days and quieter days. Or you should. If you only have quiet days, then you aren't stretching yourself enough. Go and get some more work!

If you're good and you get the message out, the work will find you. Eventually, you will have the perfect level of work.

Then you get a bit more. That bit more is one bit too much.

Some people's solution to that is to work more hours. And then you get a bit more work. Uh-oh. There are only so many hours in the day.

At some point, some of the people you are doing the work for start to

Chapter 11

realise that you haven't done what you were going to do and start chasing you. You spend a little bit of time reassuring them that all is well. Now you have a bit less time to do the work and all the other things you have to do.

It's a slippery slope.

In the case of an old boss of mine (I'll call him Fred although that wasn't his name), the amount of time spent fending people off, apologising and organising everything he needed to do kept growing until eventually it was taking up a huge chunk of his available time. The clients he was dealing with started to go from mildly impatient to really upset.

In Fred's case, one client had him by the lapels of his jacket pinned up against the wall before the other partner at the firm calmed things down.

We also had an incident where he went on holiday and one of his clients called up. This chap was standing in his house with his family when his solicitor told him that the building society weren't releasing funds for his mortgage because his accountant (Fred) still hadn't provided the reference that they'd asked for five times. All the family's possessions were on a removal van ready to move house.

Cue panic as we all went through piles of paperwork in Fred's office trying to find enough information about this client's affairs to get the reference done. It was probably the beginning of the end for Fred. Within a year, the other partners had forced him out. Despite his exceptional skills at bringing in work and giving good advice, his disorganisation was creating financial losses and dragging the firm's reputation through the mud.

Hopefully you haven't got to the point where you haven't even got time to update your to do list once a week.

Otherwise, as you finish each urgent and important task, another urgent and important task will take its place.

Everything on your to do list has a date by which it needs to be done. As

Chapter 11

you work your way through the things at the top of the list, things further down the list will be slowly getting closer to their own deadlines. That means that when you finally get to a particular task you might be very close to that task's deadline.

The task concerned will need to be done first time and correctly.

There's only one person who can do that. That's right - you!

Soon you will end up permanently drowning in urgent tasks.

But lots of the things on the list can be delegated if you're happy to accept something that's not perfect that you can then finish off.

Email is the perfect way of doing this. Pick one of the tasks further down the list, get a good Dictaphone app and start explaining what you need doing. Then ping it out.

That's you setting a hare running.

And then do another one.

Some of those hares you've set running, won't get done correctly.

Accept it.

Don't use it as an excuse to not delegate in future. At the very least, you will find out which of your team are keen to learn, which need to be trained a bit better, which need more detailed instructions and how you can improve your learning skills.

You're either winning or you're learning right?

Some of your team might actually surprise you. They'll get a lot of the work done for you and if you find a bit of time to teach them the things they didn't get right, bit by bit, they will get better at those tasks and maybe take more work off you.

Chapter 11

If I have a deadline which is weeks away, I set the hares running early. I have a look at what needs to be done and I consider who else needs to be involved. I also think about who else might be able to help me. Maybe a junior member of staff who didn't seem particularly busy and could give me some help on this.

For example, I might send an email out to somebody asking them to dig out a particular PowerPoint presentation that I did two or three years ago. I tell them what to call it and where to save it.

Two days later I get a reply. I then have a quick look at it to remind myself what was in it in the first place. Then I send another email asking if they can do some research on a particular issue and include some of that content in the PowerPoint.

A couple of days later it's back again.

What I am doing is reducing the amount of work that I am going to have to do and reducing the time pressure on getting it done.

Bit by bit, the project starts to take shape and with several days to go before the deadline it is pretty much all done. Just the finishing touches left.

For this to work, you have to be 'slightly over-staffed'. This a concept I referred to in my book Accidental Millionaires – the secret mindset successful business owners share with sporting legends.

If you're not, then you won't have capacity to take on any more work. And then you won't be able to cope with the inevitable peaks that occur from time to time.

My experience working for Fred taught me a few things. The first was that no matter how busy I am, I need to ensure that on Monday morning my to do list is bang up to date. This often requires me to find a quiet hour or two on a Saturday morning to delegate as many things as possible.

Chapter 11

Back in the 90s this involved a trip to the office and a pad of post-it notes on which I would scribble my instructions before attaching them to whatever the relevant documents were and leaving them on the desk of the person who I knew could do the work. Nowadays of course I just log on from wherever I am and start sending a few emails.

At my accountancy practice, we have tried to ensure we are slightly over-staffed by taking on new trainees each year and also by taking on staff offshore.

Most firms do neither. They think they don't need those staff and if they can't see beyond the end of their nose they are probably right. In the end, their lack of growth will (in their eyes) prove them right.

But to set the hares running requires good staff.

And good staff are hard to find.

Chapter 12

Outcome, Performance, Process

"I don't really understand," said Ruby. "I thought you were really happy. I can't understand why you'd chuck it all in to go into recruitment."

Phil sighed.

In a way he didn't understand either. He loved working at Bright Interiors. He got on well with the guys that did the work, and he knew they respected the fact that he had worked his way up, that he'd done the work they were doing, that he'd help out if a situation required it, and that he did the thing that ensured that they stayed employed, namely getting business.

Despite the abrasive manner of Ruby's oldest brother, Phil even rubbed along pretty well with Joe. In fact, their very different skills complimented each other fairly well. He got along really well with the guv'nor who'd been his been his boss since leaving school at sixteen with two GCSE's, a shaved head and absolutely no idea what he was going to do with his life.

Since then, his hair had grown, he'd got married, become a father and worked his way up through Bright Interiors until he knew everything

Chapter 12

there was to know about the industry. He'd been part of a small business success story, and it had brought him a good salary, a small but smart house in a nice part of town and a pride in his work that many of his friends who'd got jobs in banks, supermarkets, the civil service and on building sites would never have.

He sucked his top lip wondering how to explain it.

"You know Gemma works for a solicitors' in town?" he mumbled.

Gemma was Phil's former childhood sweetheart and now wife, a lively funny girl prone to the occasional gaffe after a few drinks who Ruby had met on several occasions. "Well, she was out with the girls and Ella (Dan's wife and long-time friend of Gemma) mentioned that your Dad transferred 20% of the shares each to Joe and Dan about a year ago."

Up until that point Phil had been looking been down, but now he raised his head and looked Ruby squarely in the eyes. "I'm not stupid, I don't expect to be treated like a son or anything, but it just made me realise that there's nowhere else to go in the business. Joe knows what he's doing and Dan's a good lad but I'm the one that brings in all the new customers. Sooner or later, they'll be running the place and I'll be doing exactly what I'm doing now. I just thought I needed a change."

"But recruitment!" Ruby gasped trying to lighten the mood.

"It's just a job Ruby," said Phil. "Just something to tide me over for six months until I work out what I'm going to do. I feel pretty guilty, even knowing about the shares, like it's nothing to do with me really, but I also feel a little bit let down."

Suddenly a comment that Joe had made the previous Christmas all made sense. He'd been teasing Ruby about her layabout student lifestyle but in a way that had made Ruby realise that her big brother was secretly proud that little Rubes was heading towards the first degree in the history of the Bright family.

Chapter 12

"Don't worry about stealing a bit of our inheritance" he'd joked "Cos me and Dan are gonna nick some of yours this year." It had never quite made sense at the time but now she understood.

"I guess that's the problem with family businesses." Ruby commented looking at Phil for a reaction. Phil just shrugged his shoulders. The conversation turned to more comfortable subjects of holidays and Ruby's new job before a disconsolate Ruby said her goodbyes and headed back to the office.

"Good luck with the accountants," Phil said as they headed for their cars. "Don't worry about me, I'm a big boy!"

And he was. Ruby knew that Phil would succeed whatever he did now. He was too switched on and he'd learnt a huge amount about running a business from working at Bright Interiors.

Ruby got the feeling that Phil had learnt just as much about how to avoid doing things wrong as he had about doing things right. It just seemed that a fantastic opportunity was slipping through everyone's fingers though. Phil would take years to get himself to the level of responsibility he had at the firm and Bright's would take years to find someone like Phil, if indeed they ever did.

She just didn't have a solution.

After an afternoon working on some figures for a local plumbing business, Ruby headed for home. The vans and the Tesla were back but Ruby wasn't too sure whether that meant good news.

Dinner was being served up as Ruby entered the family dining room and the mood was certainly lighter than the last time all five of them had been together.

Joe was explaining the "Outcome Performance Process" method of developing a business strategy. Mum was enthusiastically nodding, delighted at her eldest son's passion for the family business. David was

Chapter 12

smiling with the thought that the burden of running the business was finally being shared and Dan was relaxed, comfortable in letting big brother take centre stage.

The debate was more animated than usual but also calmer. Ruby sometimes had the feeling that there was an under-current in the conversations about business, like each member of the family held a secret grudge that they constantly hinted at.

Not today though. The discussions flowed around whether they should be down-sizing, whether they should think about selling up to a bigger competitor and a whole load of other issues.

They never quite reached any conclusions on anything but at least they were talking, and they seemed to have the same goals.

Ruby pondered whether to mention her discussions with Phil. It didn't seem like quite the right time, so she let the different discussions wash over her whilst she considered the best time to bring up her idea. 'Maybe not today, maybe not tomorrow, but soon' she thought using a line that her Mum liked to roll out every now and again.

Chapter 13

The Moneyball concept

If you've seen the film Moneyball but not read the book, then hopefully I can fill in a few blanks because Hollywood takes a shortcut or two when it attempts to cram 200 pages of content into a two-hour film.

As anyone who has read my book *Accidental Millionaires – the secret mindset successful business owners share with sporting legends* will know, I love sport as much as I love business. So, a book about the business of sport was always going to be hoovered up by me.

Moneyball is not just any old sports business book. Its reputation has grown so much that *Moneyball* has become such a widely used term that it has its own Wikipedia page. A place in the Oxford English Dictionary beckons.

So, a quick resume of the story in case you're not familiar. The Oaklands As are a below average US baseball team managed by an ex-pro called Billy Beane. Unable to compete with the richest clubs in the league, they are constantly looking for ways to build a winning team on a limited budget.

Chapter 13

Beane hooks up with a Harvard graduate called Paul DePodesta (although the film re-names him Peter Brand) who has created a system to identify baseball players who are under-valued. The sort of statistical analysis he utilises has been around since the 1960s but has been widely ignored by the conventional thought processes of an industry of scouts trusting their gut instinct and experience.

Beane builds a team of what might be called 'misfits' which goes on one of the longest winning runs in baseball history.

In professional sport, the Moneyball concept is widely adopted to the point where the basic statistics used by Podesta are now available to everyone. But the skills at interpreting those statistics are not universal. And those seeking sporting talent are prepared to go further and further afield to find under-valued talent.

But in your world, such statistics are not available. Your decisions about the people you pick for your organisation are driven by basic information on a cv, an interview which might last no more than two hours and perhaps (worse) a sales pitch by a recruitment agent determined to get their candidate into your company.

But like sport was in the days before Moneyball, every industry has candidates who are over-valued and candidates who are under-valued. There are no hard and fast rules on this but here are four key issues you should consider before making the next appointment:

1. **Qualifications**

   Important right? Well maybe not. Relevant qualifications demonstrate to the world that someone is capable of passing exams on whatever it is that your business does. As a result, there are now thousands of businesses who will now consider them for employment who won't consider those without the qualifications.

   The impact of that of that is that the market value of those people has gone up, but at whose expense? Well, at the expense of those who haven't passed their exams.

Chapter 13

If you did exams and qualifications yourself, think about the day you passed. Did your ability to do your job suddenly leap up? Of course not. If you're looking for value in your business, why not look for those who have not yet passed those exams or perhaps who have given up trying to pass them?

2. Full-time v part-time
There are some jobs which can't be done part-time.
But they are far fewer than most business owners will admit to.
The real reason most business owners fail to make part-time positions work in their business is because they fail to plan ahead. Decisions are made on the hoof, so discussions need to take place with colleagues there and then.

Yet they seem to be able to work around those same members going on holiday.

In the meantime, there is a whole army of people out there looking for an income that can be earned around family commitments or health issues. There is also the grey market of people with a pension or investment income not quite big enough to retire on who still want to work but not at the expense of doing the things they want to do before they are too old to do them.

Most of these people are ignored by most employers. So they seek out jobs which are at a lower level than their skills and experience would dictate. If you can just organise your business to accommodate their part-time hours you get an exceptional member of your team.

3. Experience v no experience
The reason that experience is over-valued is that most businesses fail to plan. Or they are so pessimistic about their potential that they keep their staff levels at their absolute minimum. Then when a whole load of work comes along, they need staff at short notice. Trainees or apprentices are no good in that situation. They need people who can hit the ground running.

Chapter 13

So they hire experience and in doing so, they often overlook the fact that the candidate they are hiring has gone through 5 jobs in the past 10 years. They don't pry too hard at the interview about the reasons. They probably don't want to know. *Keep your fingers crossed.*

As a result, they often take on people with bad habits or over-inflated opinions of their own skills. In short, they over-pay.

On the other hand, someone with no experience maybe straight out of school has no bad habits, is willing to learn and of course is at the bottom of the pay grade.

For it to work, you need to plan ahead (the Summer or early Autumn is the best time to recruit apprentices) and you need a training programme. At my accountancy practice, we take on 3 or 4 trainees every year, but we have a training programme which came 3rd in a national survey of training programmes for school leavers (behind Nestle and McDonalds in case you were wondering).

But you don't need an award-winning training programme. Just a recruitment model that spreads the net as wide as possible, a list of the skills that your apprentice will need to develop, someone who is willing to teach, and a review process which is a lot more regular than once a year

4. Offshore

The last category of potential employees that is widely overlooked are those who are offshore.

If the pandemic taught us anything, it is that many jobs can be done from anywhere. Yes, I can hear you thinking right now that you can't beat having everybody under one roof with the opportunities to communicate and share knowledge.

But many jobs don't need that. They just need someone who knows what they are doing, can follow the necessary processes and can get the work done.

Chapter 13

These people are not easy to find. Well not if you are only looking in your local area anyway.

But if you're prepared to go further afield where jobs are a little more scarce, there are lots of people with the right skills just waiting for the right opportunity.

Our favourite location is Durban in South Africa. Unemployment is high, qualifications are very similar to those in the UK, there is only a one-hour time difference in Summer (two in Winter) and the accent of those who speak English as their first language is mild compared to our own. Perhaps crucially, salaries are between 50% and 60% of the levels in the UK.

The over-riding theme of all four categories is that you need to be flexible. If you're not prepared to be flexible, you are fighting with all your competitors over the same dwindling pool of talent.

Chapter 14

Sliding doors

It was 11am the following morning and Matt had spent the last couple of hours running through many of the general systems in the office.

Ruby now understood about timesheets, data security and how to use the detailed systems notes. She felt that they seemed to have thought of everything and if she couldn't remember them all then once she had started work, they could all be accessed easily on the firm's Intranet.

"This must have taken ages to put together." she said

"Years. Although if I'd known then what I know now, I could have done it in half the time."

"What did you get wrong?"

"Mainly the order of things but also the way of making the systems easy to use."

"Do most firms have systems like this?"

Chapter 14

"No-one I know of. I think most practitioners are too busy to really get started on them. Chas used to say I was potty."

"He doesn't have anything like this, then?"

"No. We went in separate directions on that front really. It was a bit like that Gwyneth Paltrow movie when she misses the tube and then the film shows her life going in two different ways. What's it called?"

"Sliding doors?" Ruby responded.

"Yeah, that's it. Well, that was me and Chas. Up to Ron's heart attack, we were peas in a pod. We worked in a similar way, played the same sports, earned the same money and had similar lifestyles. I was even best man at Chas's wedding. Then, I came up here and just had a different idea about how things should be run."

"What changed?"

"Well, it was all down to one of those business gurus. A guy called Michael Gerber. I was still at Mortimore's but I'd read a few things about this guy in the business and accountancy press, mainly him going on about how small businesses don't work. What he meant was that in a small business, the owners do all the work, whereas in a larger business like McDonalds for example, the systems are so good that the business almost runs itself."

"Chas didn't believe in that then?"

"I think he would have done, but this is where it was like the film. I heard that this guy Gerber was doing a lecture in London, so I booked us up to go.

Chas was really keen and Ron didn't mind paying. He said it was too late for him to learn any new tricks but not for us. It was booked up months in advance and that's when Eric died and we did the deal with Mrs Abrahams and then Ron had his heart attack. By the time the lecture came round, the two of us were working silly hours running two different offices."

Chapter 14

"So, he cried off, but you went"

"Well guessed! Although it could have been the other way round. A few days before the lecture, I was thinking that I really had too much work to go swanning off to London to listen to some American, but I didn't want to let Chas down. Then on the day, I'm about to leave my office to drive to the station and Chas rings up and says something urgent has come up and he's not going to be able to make it."

"Sounds like it was a bit life-changing."

"It really was. Chas asked me to send him the notes, but they wouldn't have meant that much anyway. Listening to this little guy on the stage describing the way small businesses are, was hilarious. I just pictured all these clients that I knew and he was describing them to a tee."

"Is that why you started writing all these systems notes?"

"Kind of; but not for quite a while. I had all these ideas but no time to do anything about them. I'd only been in Wickfield for a few weeks, and I was just fire-fighting. There was so much to do."

"Uncle Eric always seemed so organised. I'm surprised he left things in such a mess."

"No, he was organised in his own head. As I said, I didn't know Eric, but I feel that I did. Everything I heard, convinced me that he had a giant computer inside his head. He must have done because there was nothing down on paper anywhere."

"What sort of things?"

"Everything and anything. No-one except him knew anything about the financial administration of the practice, the personal details of his clients were on various computers and even in paper files and he always preferred meeting clients to explain things rather than putting anything in writing."

Chapter 14

"That sounds like Uncle Eric. Kitty had a real job even finding out who Eric had his life insurance with. Eric took care of everything at home like that as well, I think. Mum still sees Kitty from time and I think that it took her years to be able to fend for herself after he died. She's not daft though."

"I know she isn't. She drove a hard bargain with Ron for the practice, but I think she just allowed herself to become dependent on him for loads of things."

"I kind of get the feeling you'd rather let people fend for themselves."

"Absolutely, but I don't believe in dropping people in the deep-end without swimming lessons first!"

"Which is where the systems all come in." Ruby was starting to get the hang of this place already.

"Very good. You're learning fast. But the systems are not the most important part of it. The most important part of this little lot are the roles that you occupy."

"Roles?"

"Yes. Roles. One of the things we did as the practice grew was identify all the different roles that existed in the office and then allocate them out. We found that there were almost sixty roles that existed in this office."

"But there are only 25 of you."

"Of course there are, but most people occupy several roles."

"And what about me?"

"You'll be an accounts specialist and tax return specialist for the first few months anyway. Then we'll see what you're good at and maybe give you a few more roles to occupy."

Chapter 14

"And I suppose you've got systems notes for each of these roles?"

"Oh dear, I'm becoming the sad and predictable accountant that my mates said I would become. Yes of course, we've got systems for each aspect of each of the roles. But first, Akram has said that he's going to take you to the pub on your first day. It's a bit of an office tradition and besides, he wants to get the fiver back from your family after your Dad beat him at pool during the last audit."

With perfect timing, Akram tapped on the door and put his head around.

"Ready to lose your family inheritance on the pool table?" he said. Ruby smiled. Her Dad wasn't the only one in the Bright family who was a bit of a pool hustler.

Chapter 15

Finding your invisible heroes

When you think of heroes, who would you think of as being the bigger hero? A firefighter or a health and safety officer?

Not hard to make that decision, is it?

One goes into burning buildings facing imminent danger. The other walks round with a clipboard and a checklist.

No contest.

But is that just based on your personal perception of what a hero is? Someone who runs to the rescue, preventing an imminent disaster from happening.

What if we changed our definition of hero? What if we based it on who saved the most lives?

You could easily count the number of lives a firefighter saved. It's probably in a file somewhere. The people whose life was saved will never forget the person who rescued them from a burning building.

Chapter 15

But for the Health and safety officer, we'll never know.

Because the lives they saved were saved by preventing something from happening. By ensuring that equipment was safe, that the right materials were used or that the correct lighting was installed.

There are people walking around today whose lives were saved because something didn't happen. Maybe you or your parents are alive because of something a Health and safety officer prevented.

Back in the 1980s, we had a couple of disasters every year. Kings Cross, Bradford football ground, Marchioness, Piper Alpha oil rig, Manchester airport, The Herald of Free Enterprise. They went on and on. Hundreds of people dead. Disaster became normal.

But the 90s saw a change in mindset to one that tried to prevent these things happening. Today's world is a much safer place.

In 2017, we all saw the awful impact of the Grenfell fire on our TVs. For those of us old enough to remember it was a reminder of days gone by.

But what about all the other similar buildings that had small fires which were quickly extinguished or never happened in the first place? We'll never know who ensured that all the people in those buildings were never woken by fire engines or died in their sleep of smoke inhalation. Invisible heroes.

One of my clients once said that if it wasn't for the advice he received from our firm, he might not have been around a year later – he was talking about himself not the business!

I heard an amazing line in Ricky Gervais's TV series *After Life* that 'a society grows great when old men plant trees, the shade of which they know they will never sit in'.

And maybe 'a business grows great when it's staff put things right when no-one else has noticed that they were wrong.'

Chapter 15

Of course, that's probably a big part of your job. One that few people will notice.

Some of your team will appreciate what you've done though. They're the good ones. Hang on to them. Those with the special power to see invisible heroes are often invisible heroes themselves.

Others will judge you by their own standards and assume you either did very little or simply did whatever you did for no-one but yourself.

Do you remember the 19th March 2020? I do. It was the day before the Chancellor stood up and announced The Job Retention Scheme.

One of my clients told me a story about how that day the most difficult member of his team was coming up with a whole list of jobs that they could all do while things were quiet.

My client was really surprised. He'd never seen this level of initiative from that particular employee before. He went home thinking how amazing it was that the pandemic had created a 'we're all in this together' attitude even from the most difficult employee.

And then Rishi Sunak made his announcement. And the following day the same employee demanded to be furloughed and claimed it was his right!

He was of course only ever looking out for himself. Some people always will. They can fool you for a while but their behaviour in certain situations will always give them away.

For the HR lawyers reading this, you may want to look away now or jump a few paragraphs because the next bit of advice might not be for your liking.

If you want your business to be less dependent on you, you need to try and remove some of the people like that from your business by whatever (legal) means necessary. They will drag their colleagues down and drag

Chapter 15

you down at the same time. You spend a lot of time at work. Spend it with people you like.

Because the people you need are the sort of colleagues who will choose to spent time training a junior colleague. Or editing a standard template the company uses so that customers understand it better. Or giving a great impression of your business to a potential customer even when you're not looking.

They're the sort who will ask a colleague how they're getting on, dig a little deeper and do what they can to help. They're the sort of person who refers to the company as 'we'.

You need more of these people. They are your invisible heroes.

They are all out there. Some may be feeling very unappreciated wherever they are and thinking about their next move.

If you get it right, then hopefully they will be your invisible heroes of the future. You're going to need them to make your business dependent on you.

Chapter 16

Mr Leverage and Mr Systems

Five pounds better off and watching a slightly aggrieved Akram nursing his now lighter wallet, Ruby headed back to the training room. Matt was already there loading up some more systems notes to show me.

"Good lunch?" he said.

"Not bad. Akram might be a good accountant but he's a rubbish pool player. Bit better at golf though I hear."

"Too right. He was down to a five handicap until his lady came on the scene. He keeps challenging me to play for the Wyder Cup but I'm saving that in case Chas decides to get in touch again."

"You stopped playing for it then?"

"Yeah, it was a bit strange really. I won it but I said something that perhaps I shouldn't have, and he was grumpy for the rest of the round."

"How did you offend him?"

Chapter 16

"I didn't really offend him. It was more of a case of the Emperor's new clothes."

"What do you mean?"

Bit of a long story really. Chas booked up for us to play over at Sulthorp Manor, where your Dad plays these days. As usual, he was late, so I'm in the pro shop arguing about our tee time. Chas has told me that it's booked for 2.07 but they haven't got our name down at all. Anyway, I look at the booking form and instead of Turner and Pevy it says Mr Leverage and Mr Systems."

"Right... " Ruby said uncertainly.

"Well, that was Chas's little joke. He's Mr Leverage and I'm Mr Systems."

"I see." she replied although she wasn't sure that she did.

"So he turns up and rushes onto the course and we start playing and having our usual jokes. He's totally stressed out about work of course, so I mentioned about some of our systems, and he says 'You and your bloody systems. Doesn't make you any more profitable though. You might have systems, but we make all the money'."

"Was that true?"

"Well according to our accounts, he was right. We'd both grown our businesses, but Chas had done it by buying up some of the other local firms and I'd done it by spending money on marketing, IT and systems and growing organically. We always did a comparison every year of our respective figures and Chas's business always looked more profitable. But it was only because his biggest cost was buying goodwill and that gets put on the Balance Sheet as an asset rather than getting shown as a cost."

Ruby was struggling to recall the contents of her accounting module from University, to get her head round this one but Matt ploughed on.

Chapter 16

"You see Chas had spent the best part of half a million quid buying goodwill and it appeared as an asset on his Balance Sheet. We'd spent about a third of that over the years acquiring the same amount of goodwill but because we spent the money on marketing, it got treated as a cost and made us look less profitable."

Ruby was starting to understand.

"Anyway, I blurted this out and do you know, I'm not sure if Chas had even thought it through before. He'd spent all his time buying these other practices, but he hadn't thought whether he could have done it another way."

"What happened?"

"Nothing really. It was his shot, and the conversation ended there. He was fuming though. It was like he blamed me for pointing out the obvious."

"The Emperor's new clothes!" Ruby exclaimed.

"Exactly. And of course, while he had more profit on paper, he was having to spend much of it repaying loans to the bank."

"I don't understand why Chas didn't do what you did though. Why did he keep borrowing money to buy up practices if he could have achieved the same thing by spending money on marketing?"

"Well, he could, but he didn't really have the time to get it all up and running. All the systems in our office meant that I was getting the time to put all this in place, and he didn't have time to go to the loo some days. Let me ask you a question for a change. Have you ever wondered why sometimes things never get done even though everyone knew that they needed to be done?"

"Absolutely. Sounds like Dad's place. His secretary Irene has this poster on her wall about the story of four people. Anybody, Nobody, Somebody and Everybody."

Chapter 16

"Good I'm glad you've seen it. I used to chuckle about it when I was at Levington, Philips and Bruce because it summed up the way things went wrong sometimes. We don't have that problem now though because we always try and ensure that only one person is responsible for each thing. That way no-one assumes that somebody else will do it. They know it's their responsibility to get it done so they always make sure that it is."

"What happens if they're not in?"

"If they're not in, then its their responsibility to make sure that someone is deputising for them, even if they ring in sick one day. It's been the key to the way we have been able to grow. Everyone knows what their responsibilities are, and we work really well as a team. It's also a really good way of helping our trainees (like you) to progress through the firm. As you get more experienced, you'll take on new roles and delegate some of the others to more junior members of the firm."

"And that made all the difference?"

"Absolutely. Mortimore's didn't have that. Everyone was stressed out all the time, coping with the work they already had. When they got a new client, somewhere along the line the service to another client would suffer and they'd lose them. Chas found that the only way he could grow was to buy up more practices."

"And it didn't work."

"No, it did work. He did get more leverage, and he did make bigger profits. He'll be cash rich eventually but only when he's repaid all the loans or he sells the business. He might be too old or too ill to enjoy the money though because I'm not sure he's gonna' last the pace. I certainly couldn't put up with all the stress he has."

"So, you guys fell out and stopped talking all because you pointed out the flaw in his business plan?"

"No. Chas stopped talking to me because of that young lady over there."

Chapter 16

I looked through the window to see a small blonde lady chatting to one of her colleagues. Then I turned to Matt anticipating the piece of office scandal that he was about to reveal.

"I know what you're thinking because you're a chip off the old David Bright block," said Matt "but it's nothing like that. Let me introduce you to Shona". Matt jumped up to open the door and waved Shona in. "Shona, this is Ruby Bright, David's daughter. She started here this week as our latest trainee."

"Oh no, I hope she's not like her Dad. I have enough of his awful jokes every time I ring up to get the payroll details. You better behave though." she said laughing.

"Shona. Can you spend the next hour running through the basics of the Accounts Specialist role. I've got a couple of calls to return. Ruby, when I'm back, we're going to run through communicating with clients and more importantly I'm going to tell you how this young lady caused two best mates to fall out."

Matt looked at Shona and grinned. Shona just rolled her eyes in a way that indicated that she'd heard this story many times before.

Section C
Boring Is under-rated

Chapter 17

Sloping shoulders and monkey collectors

Whilst building my accountancy practice, I've also built up a small portfolio of flats with a business partner.

If ever we have an empty property leading up to Christmas, I always joke that we will get a tenant in the New Year as couples often split up in January. Perhaps it's all that talk of resolutions that causes people to make a big change in their lives! Even if it's not as drastic as that, the gyms and weight-watchers classes are always full!

But change doesn't always need to be as big as starting again or going on drastic fitness programmes!

Most changes are incremental. Imagine flying a helicopter and moving the control stick by one degree. Then 5 minutes later by another degree and 5 minutes later by another. These are small changes but do that for an hour and you will end up in a completely different place than the one you would have reached.

Even if your business has been going for decades, that doesn't mean you can't improve and there will be loads of areas which are not as effective

Chapter 17

as others. Even if you were perfect, some new technology will come along and move the goalposts.

Back in the dim and distant past, I had a difficult manager who was always telling everyone how important she was and never admitting to making any mistakes even though they were obviously her fault. For the purposes of this email, we will call her Tina although that wasn't her real name.

I also had a lady who did a variety of admin and financial jobs who we'll call Shirley.

Shirley was one of the most conscientious people who ever worked for the firm. She eventually retired through ill-health many years after the normal retiring age.

Shirley rarely said anything bad about anyone so when she made a comment in a discussion about Tina having 'sloping shoulders', I asked her what she meant.

"Well," she explained, "everything that's on her shoulders seems to slide right off them and across the desk to Jemima." Again, Jemima wasn't her real name, but she was a very good junior member of staff who became a very good senior member of staff in the years that followed.

I made a point to keep an eye on the situation and observed over the next few weeks how little actual work Tina did. Even the things that she was qualified to do, and Jemima wasn't, seemed to end up being done by Jemima.

The final straw was when some work that I'd given Tina was wrong and Tina blamed Jemima! That's what people with sloping shoulders do.

Of course, the opposite of sloping shoulders are monkey collectors. This is covered in the book *The One Minute Manager Meets the Monkey*.

In the book, the writer encourages the reader to think of each task that

Chapter 17

needs to be done as a monkey. If you've got to do it, then you have a monkey on your back.

In your business, generally speaking, the main monkey collectors are also great staff members.

As the business owner, you want your apprentices to become great monkey collectors. You want them to take every single monkey they can get. You want them to be hungry to learn new things.

What you don't want is for them to become barriers to growth.

The more monkeys someone has dealt with, the more experience they will have gained and the more valuable they will be as an employee – until they get too many monkeys of course.

This happens when an inbox is full to bursting. When they don't even have enough time to keep their 'to do' list up to date. At that point, monkey collecting habits start to cause a few problems alongside the raft of solutions they usually provide.

Time to do something.

Getting the balance right between sloping shoulders and monkey collectors is a challenge in every business.

The long-term solution requires complete clarity on who is responsible for what. There are six stages to this:
1. Identify all the roles that exist within your organisation and document them in an index of roles
2. Identify which are primary roles i.e. must only be occupied by one person and which are multi roles
3. Allocate each of the Primary roles to a member of the team
4. Identify the members of staff who fill all the multi-roles
5. Work out which role reports to which other role starting with Managing Director and working outwards
6. Train them on those roles

Chapter 17

What that 6-step process does is create *total clarity*.

That will reduce the risk of sloping shoulders and stop the conscientious monkey collectors from drowning in things that should be done by someone else.

Of course, those with sloping shoulders will immediately be thinking how to get round your big initiative.

One way to stop that happening is to put a pack together for each member of staff including all the roles they do. Then ask them to sign under each role page that they will undertake that role to the best of their ability. People with sloping shoulders hate this because they know it's harder to wriggle off the hook.

When we did that at our accountancy firm, it was a fantastic exercise. Those who were happy that they understood the roles they had on their staff page, signed immediately. Those who had a few things on their roles that they'd never had proper training on, let us know which bits they needed help on, and we got it organised.

One person who was determined not to do their job and was a walking 'disaster magnet' left.

A few of the sloping shoulder brigade, dragged their heels, came up with nonsensical excuses that evolved into some unambiguous conversations that needed to be had.

It was a good result all round.

Chapter 17

The TV writer Charles Osgood wrote a poem about responsibility which illustrates the importance of getting people to understand the responsibilities of their roles:

This is a story about four people named Everybody, Somebody, Anybody and Nobody.
There was an important job to be done and Everybody was sure that Somebody would do it.
Anybody could have done it, but Nobody did it.
Somebody got angry about that, because it was Everybody's job.
Everybody thought Anybody could do it, but Nobody realized that Everybody wouldn't do it.
It ended up that Everybody blamed Somebody when Nobody did what Anybody could have.

The story may be confusing, but the message is clear: no one took responsibility, so nothing got accomplished.

It's a story that plays out often in organisations and companies and in teams - anywhere there is a culture that lacks accountability.

Get the roles properly documented, allocated and trained and then the story of Everybody, Somebody, Anybody and Nobody won't happen in your company. Shoulders won't be quite so sloping and you won't have as many of good members of staff collapsing under troops of monkeys.

Chapter 18

Systems and admin

I'm sure like me you've had one of those days on holiday when it's mid-afternoon and you suddenly feel the overwhelming desire for a snooze. Put the book down, pull down the baseball cap and have yourself forty winks.

Afterwards, I always question how I can be so tired. I always have an hour's extra sleep per night when on holiday (at least) and its not as if I'm doing anything strenuous.

And before you make the assumption that its down to too many cans of Red Stripe from the all-inclusive bar, I've discounted that one as it also happens on days when I haven't indulged, as well as those when I have.

A friend of mine explained this phenomenon.

It's all to do with unfamiliar places and routines.

You see, human beings are creatures of habit. We are internally programmed to prefer routine. Think about all the things that you do every day which are the same as the previous day and the day before that.

Chapter 18

You get out of the same side of the bed, brush your teeth over the same sink using the same toothbrush. You prepare your breakfast in the same kitchen, possibly having the same breakfast cereal bought from the same shop. You get into a car you've driven every day for a few years, listen to a radio station you usually listen to and drive a route to work you've done a few hundred times.

Imagine if all those things were completely different every day. Different bed, different kitchen, different car, different route to work.

You'd be exhausted before you even made it to the office.

But also imagine that everything for the entire day was the same - absolutely everything. Not just your morning routine but the work you do, the people you speak to, the food you eat, even the TV programmes you watch in the evening.

How soul-destroying would that be?

As human beings, we are programmed such that routine makes us comfortable, but differences make us alive. 'Vive la différence' as the French would say. 'A change is as good as a rest' as my old Nan used to say.

Getting that balance right between the routine and the new is the key to a successful business and career. "Systemise the 90% so you can humanise the 10%" is one of my favourite work expressions.

Ok; so this is where I get to summarise a big chunk of my career in a few paragraphs. I'm going to explain how to write a system.

DO NOT SKIP THIS BIT.

Yes, it's boring. But if you want to be a little bit less Elton and a little bit more Ronald, then you need to know how to write a system. It's easier than you think. Just follow this guide:

Chapter 18

1. **Name the system**
   This should be something that simply describes what you are doing in concise terms. Let's pick something we all do every day: Getting dressed for work.

2. **Identify whose responsibility it is**
   Sometimes this will be something that only one person does i.e. it is part of a Primary role (see previous chapter). Or it might be something that lots of people do as is the case in this example. So, we would say something like: 'This task is the responsibility of everyone who has a job.'

3. **Explain the purpose**
   The purpose might be obvious but you should still explain it. The purpose is not what you are doing but why you are doing it. You might write something like 'The purpose of this task is to ensure you are dressed appropriately for the current weather conditions and look presentable to those you will come into contact with in your working day.'

4. **Set out the trigger**
   This is what has caused you to find yourself in the position of needing to do this task. It could be driven by a time of the day or week 'this task is undertaken every weekday apart from when I am on holiday' or it may follow a previous task 'this task arises immediately after eating breakfast' or perhaps it is driven by outside forces 'this task occurs when I hear my mother shouting 'you're going to be late'.

5. **Write a checklist of the key steps in numbered form**
   These are the individual steps that you will need to do in order to complete the task e.g. 1. Remove Harry Potter pyjamas, 2. Get boxer shorts from drawer, 3. Put boxer shorts on 4. Decide on appropriate suit etc. The checklist is there to help ensure that those who essentially know what they are doing don't forget any key steps.

6. **Write a detailed explanation of each step**
   Under each numbered point set out how you do each of those points

Chapter 18

step by step. For example, deciding on an appropriate suit as mentioned above might be something like: a. Look at diary to see if you have any meetings with clients today b. assess weather conditions c. Review if any suits need to go to dry cleaning etc. This detail is there for training purposes when someone new is stepping into the role that uses this system. It will also be used by them to refer back to after training

7. **Identify the next stage in the process**
   This is really important because whilst it is not part of this system it is a big part of the reason why you are doing this system. After getting dressed for work, the next system might be driving to work. If you don't have any shoes on because the system didn't include that then your feet might slip off the pedals causing you to crash. Eventually, you will have a collection of systems that all link seamlessly together.

Whilst the example referred to above may be simplistic enough to not need to be written down, most of the systems in your business are not as simple. How many times have you found yourself debating with a member of staff whether you told them something that they believe was never mentioned but you believe they have forgotten? Writing it down means there is a document to refer to. They know it's there. You know it's there and they know that you know that they know it's there. No more excuses.

Yay! The most important lesson of the book is done. Everything will fine.

Well of course its more complicated than that. It always is.

Your first version of the systems might look great on paper. But when it comes to doing the job, I suspect those required to follow it might find it lacks a bit of detail. In the amazing book The Toyota Way, there are lots of references to the importance of 'going to the place where the work is done'.

In practice, that means working your way through the process as if you had never done it before. That's when you find that you're missing key

Chapter 18

bits of information or that the process isn't in the right order.

You'll also need to learn how to deal with things that go wrong. We'll cover than in chapter 22.

And now for some admin.

The best systems will still fail if the environment they work in is chaotic or illogical.

The more chaotic or illogical the environment is, the more complicated the systems will need to be to cope with it. There are a few simple things you can do to make life much easier though including:
- A central document storage system for all correspondence about customers and suppliers. Ideally, this should be cloud based or at least on a server that key members of staff can access so your team can work from remote locations if required.
- A reliable database system that centralises all information about customers and potential customers.
- An agreed format for naming files. We prefer to give all files (apart from systems and templates) a file name that starts with the date in the following format YYYY.MM.DD followed by a description of the file. That way it's easy to find later. Different versions just get given later dates so everyone knows which is the later version
- A password protected directory for staff information. Again, this should be cloud-based.

There are many pieces of software that will do much of the above but don't rely on the software to set the protocols that operate around them. That's not the software company's job, it's yours!

But of course, just as an exceptional employee can operate well in even the most dysfunctional environment, an incompetent employee can mess up the best system in the world. Time to bring in the humans.

Chapter 19

Are we human or are we dancers?

First of all, apologies to the Killers fans who spotted the deliberate error in the above title. The grammar pedant in me just couldn't let it go.

If you're not familiar with The Killers, they are a stadium filling US Indie rock band led by charismatic most well-dressed man in rock, Brandon Flowers. The title of this (one of their most iconic songs) was actually stolen from a 1970s book called 'Fear and Loathing in Las Vegas' by one of America's most famous authors, Hunter S Thompson.

Born in 1937 and a heavy drug user, Thompson disdainfully criticised the next generation by suggesting that they were simply dancing to a tune written by someone else. It's easy to do that when you earn lots of money for writing slightly crazy books whilst mostly being stoned!

We all live our lives balancing the routine and the unique activities in them.

There are people in parts of the world whose lives are one of drudgery with every day repeating the other.

Chapter 19

On the other hand, a friend who is a is a social worker has a job where she finds herself sometimes having to deal with people who live chaotic lives with no routine, bouncing from one crisis to the next.

I'm not sure which is worse.

If you run your own business, you are probably lucky enough to have a good degree of balance within your work. But if you want to make it less dependent on you, then you need to always strive to systemise the 90% in order that you can humanise the 10%.

I talk about the 90% a lot. I try my best to pass on best practice to my team whenever I can. I tinker around under the hood, trying to get us to be more efficient, better, more scalable, less stressful for everyone.

It's intellectually stimulating but also hard work. I keep my fingers crossed that enough of them will meet that challenge head on as well and will in turn keep striving for best practice and passing it on to colleagues.

Of course, in your business you will be on your own journey and the likelihood is that you are nowhere near (yet) getting to a situation where 90% of the activities in your business are systemised. For the sake of this chapter, you'll need to assume that you are though. And if not, then when I talk about 'the 10%', I'm talking about the most interesting 10% of what you do.

Got that? Great, then let's talk about the 10%.

You may have worked out that I love the 10% as much as I love tinkering with the systems of the 90%. The phone call from a client about a problem or an opportunity. The human bit.

One of my partners (Emma White) who I have watched grow up from a lively teenage girl on her first day in a full-time job into a highly professional adviser with a client base who hang on her every word, described her way of looking after clients like this:

Chapter 19

"It's generally better to over-communicate. If you wait to reply because you don't have an answer yet (or because you don't want to share bad news), the other party often ends up making assumptions about what the delayed reply might mean. Silence frustrates and confuses people. Better to communicate early and often."

Communication is one of the things that makes us human. It's an art and not a science.

When our trainees start with us, one of the things they do is call up clients chasing either tax records or approval of tax returns. There are some pretty standard responses that they get, and we have documented them in the systems and train them on how to deal with those standard responses.

But there will be all sorts of things that are not standard. You can only systemise communication so far.

Sometimes there are difficult people to deal with. Sometimes there are nice people dealing with difficult circumstances that you must speak to. Sometimes there are clients suffering the early stages of dementia. There are hundreds of situations and thousands of questions. There comes a point where you have to just get on with it.

If your staff deal with the standard stuff well, the client will respect them. If they deal with the non-standard stuff well, the client will love them.

A few years ago, one of my clients described one of our then tax juniors (Kyra) as "delightful". It was definitely the non-standard stuff that elicited that compliment but if Kyra hadn't been able to deal with the standard stuff well, the client would have been so irritated by then, that Kyra's delightfulness would have been downright annoying.

It doesn't matter how good your staff are technically, at whatever it is that your company does. If they can't communicate their knowledge, you will lose out to competitors who are much less knowledgeable. Get it

Chapter 19

right, and your customers will stay with you for decades, refer you to their friends and family and forgive you on the rare occasions you don't get things 100% right.

So much for where you staff need to be though. The question is how are you going to get them there? There are a few key elements to this:

1. Develop a customer-focussed culture
2. Inductions
3. Reinforce the message regularly
4. Probation periods
5. Regular training

Let's go through these one by one.

Developing a customer-focussed culture

Many organisations operate in a hierarchical way. Usually whoever is on the higher salary wins most debates.

But in a customer-focussed business, everyone is required to think about who their customer really is. For those who deal directly with the business's customers, their customer is the same as the business's customers.

For those in support roles, their customers may be the staff who deal with the customers directly.

Then there are roles who have customers who are in other support roles. They support someone who supports someone else who provides a service to the customer of the business.

Take that logic far enough and you realise that for much of your time as Managing Director (or whatever your title is), your customers (not the firm's customers) are actually your workforce.

You didn't realise you were working for them, did you?

Chapter 19

This sort of thought process helps settle a lot of arguments about how to tackle particular issues in your business and creates a way of thinking that enables your team to make the right decisions without you.

Inductions:
Inductions for new staff are critical to getting staff off on the right foot.

This is especially important if you are making changes and getting rid of some bad apples. The new staff need to understand what you are expecting from them. This might even require you to explain to the new staff some of the problems you have had in the past.

One of the issues we explain to our staff is a funny little 'rule' that if three people want to go out to lunch together they have to invite the whole office. We explain that the reasons are to avoid cliques developing that exclude some people. It's a really symbolic issue to us and important that it's explained right at the outset. New staff always accept it because they understand the reasons.

But of course, an induction is about more than cliques. It's about the standards you expect.

If you have delegated the induction to someone else, make sure there's a system for it. Otherwise, the most important moment in that new employee's career at your company is in the hands of someone else.

Reinforce the message regularly:
Don't think you can just come up with one initiative that sets the rules for ever.

Cultures evolve and can evolve into something a long way from what you want it to be. Silence from you creates a vacuum and other voices will fill that vacuum.

If you're not careful, your new member of staff will experience a day of high-quality training in their first day induction followed by a second day observing all their colleagues doing the job in a completely different way.

Chapter 19

You will need to keep reinforcing the message, praising those you catch doing things right and intervening when you spot people not doing it right.

Probation periods:
These are critical. As we know, people can talk a good talk in interviews but don't always do what they say, or what you want them to do once they are in the job.

Probation periods should ideally be set at 6 months and can be extended if you feel someone is not working out but might be able to turn things round.

Don't be frightened to finish someone's probation early if they are doing well or let them go if you don't think they can do it. Both tactics will send out the right message to your team and encourage the right behaviour.

Regular training:
Laws change, industries change, and customers will come and go.

A regular or even an ad-hoc training programme will keep your team energetic, customer-focussed and ready to help drive the company forward.

Get all this in place and whilst you won't have managed to control the uncontrollable, you will have maximised the amount of influence it is possible to achieve.

So, are we human or are we dancers?

We're both Brandon, we're both.

Chapter 20

A helping non-human hand

'A computer once beat me at chess, but it was no match for me at kick-boxing' Emo Phillips.

Ok, let's hold my hands up on this one straight away. I am not high tech in any way, shape or form. Many conversations about technology go straight over my head.

I do get asked lots of IT questions by clients though. My usual answer when someone asks me how we do something is 'I'll ask Pete'.

Pete has worked with me for 30 years.

When we were both much younger and had more hair, I said to Pete that there was no budget for IT. It wasn't what it cost, it was what the Return on Investment was. If the return justified the investment, I would find the money. But on the other hand, no matter how small the cost, I wouldn't put my hand in my pocket if I couldn't see the return.

Chapter 20

Back then, my personal goals were all about growth and profit. Although assessing that return is hard, at least you only need to consider financial issues when making that decision.

But then of course you get a bit more successful, and profit isn't as important. Time becomes more important to you.

Now your decisions on IT take on some different considerations. Here are the things you should be thinking about if you want to use IT to make your business less dependent on you:
- Can computers control the process?
- Can you build your knowledge into your IT processes?
- Can customer service be improved?
- What can be automated?
- Artificial intelligence

Computers controlling the process?
A word of warning. We're all familiar with David Walliams' character Carol Beer in the "computer says no" sketches of Little Britain.

And we're all familiar with that feeling of frustration when something that seems quite logical can't be done because it's not an option on the IT system or app you are using!

But unless you are prepared to spend your 40s, 50s and 60s regularly looking over the shoulder of members of your staff to check they are doing something right, then you are going to have to rely on a computer programme to prevent all sorts of errors happening.

Of course, there may be an amazing piece of software out there which has thought all this through for you. Or at least that's what you're told when you buy it. Once it's installed you find out that it needs a lot more setting up than you realised and doesn't actually automate everything you thought it would.

Significant research is required if that's the route you want to go down. Firstly, get a free trial. If the software company won't allow that, don't buy. They're hiding something that they don't want you to know.

Secondly, find someone else that uses it. As exciting as it is to be an early adopter (IT industry code for 'guinea pig to find all the faults we haven't'), it really doesn't pay to be one. Let other companies in your industry test the software first. If you don't know anyone who uses it, ask the software company to put you in touch with someone who does. Again. If they won't do that, don't buy.

Building your knowledge into your IT processes
The degree to which you can do this depends on whether you are developing something yourself or buying an off the shelf package.

If you're developing yourself, you have complete control over the way the product works and every aspect. Beware of being too innovative though. Will you get a return on your investment? It's easy to spend vast sums on programmers but you can then find yourself dependent on them for every minor change.

And don't try and convince yourself that this package you've developed is so good that you will be able to sell it to others in your industry. That involves setting up an entirely new operation using all sorts of skills your business probably doesn't have. It will often end up diverting you away from whatever it is that your business does that earns the money and which you're good at.

My advice would be to find an off the shelf package that can be tailored. Fields can be added, maybe extra functions created. Use all the skills and knowledge about the best way to deliver the process to adapt questions, set parameters.

Then create a user manual that sets out how you want your staff to use the package which is maybe not the way the software compare you bought it from envisaged.

Chapter 20

Can customer service be improved?
In all of this, don't forget that the main aim of your chosen IT solution is probably to improve customer service (even if it's a supply side package there will still be implications for how you deliver your product or service to your customers).

The software might help you reduce costs and even the size of labourforce you have but if that is at the cost of customer service, you will lose business and possibly damage your reputation.

Worse, customers will come to you grumbling about falling service standards, which isn't very *less dependent*.

What can be automated?
Automation is the dream of course. Lots of activity being conducted for your business without a human in sight.

But automation needs to be vigorously tested.

We had a very cumbersome new client process that we followed which one of our managers decided could be streamlined with a bit of coding on our database.

This manager fell in the 'throw it at the wall and hope it will stick' school of change and did not take the time to look at the detail of every aspect of our cumbersome manual process to ensure that his fabulous automated process covered all the key issues. Of course, the design took much longer (and cost a lot more money) than he'd originally estimated so to save time he dispensed with any testing of the programme.

Eventually through trial and error (lots of errors), we got the thing to work. Unfortunately, it took between 18 months and 2 years before the automated version was as good as the manual version.

Artificial intelligence
Whatever I write on this subject will probably be out of date by the time I publish so I'm not going to even try.

Chapter 20

In preparation for this chapter of the book, I went onto ChatGPT and asked the question "How can I use artificial intelligence to make my business less dependent on me?".

The answer that came back was a fantastic checklist of issues that we should probably look into. I could ask another ten questions based on the contents of the answers I got.

If I asked the same question in a month's time, I suspect that I'd get an even better set of answers.

The point is that this is changing all the time.

Maybe AI will create solutions that will enable you to sit at home watching the money rolling in without lifting a finger.

Or maybe it will make it ridiculously easy for your customers to do for themselves whatever it is that you do for them consigning your business to the history books.

But let's assume that it's somewhere in between, otherwise there's not much point reading the rest of the book is there?

Chapter 21

The three reasons things go wrong

Students of history will know that the last US President to be forced from office was Richard Nixon in 1974 after the so-called Watergate scandal. It's also why every scandal these days always has a 'gate' added to the end of it by the press.

Anyway, you may also know that it wasn't the actual act which did for Nixon (aka Tricky Dicky) but the cover-up.

I thought of this during the Pandemic when I read a story about how New Zealand brought in the military to deal with a Covid-19 outbreak involving two people. Two!

New Zealand were on top of the Covid outbreak from day one which is why they managed to get life returned to normal quicker than almost every other country in the world.

But when they got it wrong, they were all over it. They didn't treat it like a minor indiscretion to be ignored or excused. They called in the military! They catastrophised about the consequences of the mistake but there was no throwing blame around. They just learned from it and acted quickly.

Chapter 21

The alternative would have been to come up with excuses. Or just hide the failure.

Both of those alternatives are pretty standard human nature approaches which is a shame because opportunities to learn are missed when you do that.

Owning up to mistakes requires humility. In the UK, we have a mixed history amongst our leaders. Margaret Thatcher and Gordon Brown could never admit to a mistake. Tony Blair and David Cameron seemed to find it much easier. Noticeably, there is no political characteristic there. Thatcher and Cameron were conservatives. Blair and Brown were Labour. It's not political, it's personality, I guess.

But I know which personality I'd prefer at my accounting practice, A4G. That's partly because A4G is all about growth and learning from mistakes.

We've even built an entire infrastructure (documented systems) where we can put all of the lessons we have learned, into a process that ensures that future staff will all learn from the mistakes of the past.

That infrastructure requires everyone to care for it and to be committed to learning from mistakes although that's not always the case.

For instance, we have what are called billing sheets which show the amount of time spent on a particular piece of work. But when a particular problem arose and I went looking for some answers I found out that if you were to summarise the reasons for losses on our billing sheets, you'd probably find it was the greatest volume of fiction since they released a box set of the Harry Potter books.

There was almost an unwritten system for doing this. Hide the loss this year, carrying time forward and then excuse next year's loss by blaming it on too much time being carried forward last year. Brilliant. No-one is to blame. Nothing to see here. Keep on walking.

That's a shame because again, the opportunity to learn from losses had been missed. And that meant that those losses continued for a lot longer than they should have.

Then there are the explanations which are completely correct, but nothing is done about them. A general apportionment of blame without ever taking the time to explain to the person who has made the mistake what they got wrong.

We say that there are only three reasons something goes wrong and there are different actions required depending on which of those three apply. The three reasons and their actions are:

1. Someone didn't follow the system
If that's the reason, then you need to politely remind them of the importance of following the system. At A4G, our employment contracts state that the member of staff will follow the documented processes. Sometimes you get an employee who feels that they are better than the system and don't need to use it. If that's the case, then you will need to escalate the issue. Gentle encouragement gives way to serious reminders which give way to verbal then written warnings. Escalate the issue until sometimes you escalate someone out the door although hopefully that is very rare.

2. Someone didn't understand the system
This is a training issue usually. If that's the case, you need to revisit the training and provide better explanations. Not everyone gets it the first time. Be patient.

3. The system wasn't good enough
The simple answer here is that the system needs to be improved. Perhaps the system is not fit for purpose or maybe it's just one minor tweak that's required.

Human nature is such that people will always try and steer it to the third one. They don't have to take the blame, and they don't have to risk confrontation by blaming someone else. But even if there is a small issue with the systems, the other two might apply as well.

Chapter 21

If you've managed to make your business less dependent on you, then you might not become aware of some of the things going wrong in your business. There could be a whole issue occurring that doesn't reach you until it's almost at disaster stage. Widget-gate!

That's why it's important to encourage the members of your team who are at the end of a process to notice the things that are wrong and do something to ensure that these things don't go wrong again.

So, who are these people at the end? Well let me give you a few examples:

- **Anyone involved in credit control.** If there is a problem getting paid, then there is usually something your firm could have done differently earlier on. Is the problem specific to this customer or a much deeper problem? Maybe it goes right back to your new customer onboarding process.

- **Senior staff reviewing work.** If it has to be changed is it because the person who did it, did a poor job? If so, they need to be told. Or is because a standard letter was at fault? In which case, get it changed.

- **Admin staff sending completed work out the door.** Sometimes there are errors in customer details which indicate the data is not right on the database. If so, they need to get it fixed on the database or the same thing will go wrong next time as well.

I could go on because there are hundreds of these opportunities. Ultimately, pretty much any of your managers are at the end of some kind of process. The trick is getting them to care enough that they all contribute to making these improvements.

Here's a technique to teach your team for handling things that have gone wrong:

1. Get the facts. What's happened and what are the consequences? Are there any other aspects to the problem that you have yet to uncover?

Chapter 21

2. What is the impact and who is affected?

3. Have you uncovered the full extent of the problem? Maybe double-check the work to make sure that there are no other problems within it.

4. Take responsibility for what went wrong. This doesn't mean that you intentionally did it wrong, or that doing it right was part of your job description. It means that you know something went wrong, you're unhappy about it and you accept responsibility for letting it get past you. Plus, you accept responsibility for making sure it won't happen again.

5. Come up with a plan to limit the impact of the problem. If you can't come up with a plan, say so and ask colleagues for suggestions.

6. Alert the relevant parties and if necessary, apologise. Not because it's your fault, but because the incident cost other people time or money or upset them and you're sorry that they have to deal with that.

7. Consider whether the problem is systemic? You may have uncovered one issue affecting one customer, but does it affect lots of others? Come up with a plan to avoid the problem in the future.

8. Identify which (and it may be more than one) of the three reasons above was the cause of the problem.

9. Act accordingly.

Whatever you do, don't have some knee-jerk reaction to the problem and get all stroppy about it. The next time a problem arises, that will only encourage your team to hide, muddy the waters, blame someone else, depersonalise and then move on to the next disaster.

Many years ago, one of the little side businesses that are part of A4G was really struggling. One problem after another - credit notes to customers

Chapter 21

where work was not done to a high enough standard, massive write-offs on jobs that had gone completely awry.

We brought in a bit of a heavy-hitter to sort it out.

And results turned round. Suddenly things looked good. The heavy-hitter worked really hard. We breathed a sigh of relief.

Then our heavy-hitter went on maternity leave. After which results went back to exactly where they were before.

Because nothing had really changed. All that had happened was that a highly effective individual had taken charge for a while and the business became them. Their strengths became the business's strengths and once those strengths were gone, we went back to the beginning.

A different heavy-hitter took charge. Me.

There was no-one else. And I didn't have the time to work really hard on this business. I had too much work to do on our main business. A different approach was required.

This is what I did.

First of all, I insisted we had really good reporting. I made sure that a junior member of the finance team sent weekly emails on how much time was spent on client work and most importantly the recovery rate on each piece of work.

In a service business, there are two main Key Performance Indicators.

First is the percentage of time you workforce spends doing work for customers.

Second is the percentage of that wok that ends getting billed to those customers. This is called your recovery rate.

Chapter 21

If you can measure them, recovery rates will highlight problem customers or problem work.

But there's no point just rubbing your hands and fretting about it. Don't suffer from paralysis by analysis. Do something with the information you get.

Each invoice with a poor recovery rate must be investigated. Something has gone wrong and as all my fellow systems-anoraks know, there are only three reasons that something goes wrong.

When I found that someone didn't follow the systems, I gave them a one-minute reprimand about the importance of following the systems.

If they didn't understand the system I gave them more training.

When the systems weren't good enough, I improved them.

Again. And again. And again.

Very boring.

Except the result isn't boring. The team (which were fairly junior and relatively inexperienced) became a lot less stressed than they were before. And they were happier that they weren't getting moaned at or moaned about by colleagues or customers.

They found they had more time to speak to clients. To answer their questions. Maybe even be a bit more pro-active and promote extra services or products.

The business you end up with and the degree to which it is reliant on you is an accumulation of the way you deal with errors and failure.

Chapter 22

The muddy bit in the middle

A couple of years' ago, two of my colleagues and I ran a 10k race at a reservoir called Bewl Water.

I wasn't due to run it, but a couple of things changed socially, and it all worked so I signed up with only two days to go. I skim read the details online. I'm sure the word 'flat' was mentioned somewhere and there was definitely the word 'path' in there.

I've done plenty of 10k runs. What else did I need to know?

At the time I was nowhere near my personal best times, but I'd done one a few weeks earlier, so my aim was simply to beat the time I did that day.

At the start line though, doubts started to kick in. I could see a big hill and the starter was talking about being careful because of how slippery it was.

'Never mind', I thought 'I've been here before. Let's get going'.

Chapter 22

I always carry my phone when I run these days. I can see my pace and whether I'm on target or not.

Off we went.

After a few hundred yards of mostly shallow downhill, my pace was, of course, well ahead of schedule. A few hundred yards later after a long hill, I was well behind.

At the bottom of the hill, I found myself running next to a lady wearing a top with my running club's name on it although in different colours. I said something to her about "glad to see another Istead and Ifield member" but she looked at me strangely and said something that didn't sound like it was in English. People do talk gibberish on long races but not usually at the start. Maybe she was some kind of imposter.

I pulled away.

The race was an out and back meaning that you get to see the leaders coming back the other way. There are usually some pretty fit runners, so I was surprised to see the leader when I was at the 2.5 mile mark meaning they were only a mile ahead of me. Strange I thought.

I turned off the road onto a muddy path. Nothing tricky. Just narrow.

Then I turned another corner, and I saw it. The quagmire. A 30-yard stretch of thick wet mud with footprints ankle deep.

Decision time.

There was no good outcome here but there were some really bad ones. My decision to carry my phone was starting to look like a bad one. If I fell over in this stuff, I might never see my phone again. I took a line of least resistance to the right and then halfway through realised that the mud was even thicker than going through the middle.

I made it though.

Chapter 22

And then another quagmire. And a third.

Annoyingly, somewhere along the way the Imposter took a better route than me and was now at least 50 yards ahead.

Eventually I was through it all. But of course, this was an out and back course. I had to do all this in reverse.

It was easier the second time. My running shoes were already covered in mud, and I knew which routes to avoid.

As I exited the last quagmire, I saw my colleagues coming the other way. I tried to think of some inspirational advice I could give them. Maybe I should write a system. "The purpose of this task is to not fall flat on your face and get covered head to toe in mud". There was nothing I could say though. There wasn't enough time. They'd have to work it out on their own. Which they did.

You might not have run a 10k recently or ever for that matter but you will have had something in your work or private life that you underestimated. The very British expression for this is 'biting off more than you can chew'.

It might even happen this week. You start on a piece of work that you thought was fairly easy, but you get stuck on the muddy bit in the middle. It turns out to be far more complicated than you were expecting. You don't know which direction to go.

Of course, you have a few choices whether it's a piece of work or a muddy 10k.

You could give up. You could get someone else to do it for you. You could just pretend the challenge didn't exist. You could put it off until tomorrow. At which point you will probably put it off again. And again.

Or you can break it down into bite size chunks and take it one step at a time.

Chapter 22

The end result might not be what you hoped for.

In the case of my 10k, I realised pretty early on that my aim to beat my previous time wasn't going to happen. So I re-set my goals.

One quagmire at a time. Once I'd made it back on dry land so to speak, I set new goals. One by one I overtook many of the people who had overtaken me in the muddy bit. With a mile to go I edged past The Imposter. In the finishing straight I gave it one last push.

The time was, of course, awful. A full 7 minutes slower than the one I'd run a few weeks earlier. I'd tested myself though and stretched my fitness. Maybe lost a pound or two in weight.

As I washed the mud off my running shoes, I resolved to be better prepared next time. Maybe check the route better and the impact of the weather not just on the day but in the days leading up to it. Perhaps buy myself some trail running shoes (designed for muddy conditions).

All business owners hit a muddy patch at some point.

One client discovered a mechanical fault in their product which resulted in almost £2m of work to recall machines and fix them. It wiped out his profit that year and the year before. But three years later, he sold his company for £20m. Success is not just about maximising the positives, it's about minimising the negatives. Better times will come.

The same thing will happen as you try to make your business less dependent on you. A system that you relied upon will fail. A member of staff you thought could trust will leave and you'll uncover a whole load of things they'd been doing incorrectly.

That's the big scale. On the smaller scale, you will have plenty of muddy patches to negotiate this month, this week, maybe even today. And when you turn the corner and discover a quagmire that you weren't expecting, re-think your plan in order to minimise your losses, re-set your goals,

Chapter 22

break the problem down into small pieces and squelch your way through until you're back on the right path.

Section D
The light at the end of the tunnel

Chapter 23

Growing pains

An hour or so later and Shona had finished showing Ruby the accounts systems. It would take many months for her to confidently be able to prepare a set of accounts on behalf of one of Abraham and Co's clients but at least she knew how this role fitted into the rest of the office.

Shona was explaining how the amount of work on this particular role depended significantly on how well the client kept their records and the training and support they gave those clients when Matt put his head around the door.

"Not scared her off yet, Shona?" he said.

"I tried but she seems to be a glutton for punishment. I think I'll enjoy having Ruby working here. Every time her Dad takes the Mickey out of me, I'll be twice as horrible to her."

"Hardly fair!" Ruby protested and Shona laughed.

"I've got to go now," said Shona "or the school will get social services on to me for abandoning my daughter. Shona smiled and left."

Chapter 23

"Shona's part-time I take it?" Ruby asked.

"Yes," said Matt, "we've got quite a few part-timers here. There's several you haven't met yet. Some are Mums like Shona, but we've got a couple with other jobs, two who are semi-retired and one who runs his own business."

"It must be difficult to get continuity with so many part-timers." Ruby commented.

"No, not really. You see they all know what their roles are and just as importantly, we all know what their roles are. There are one or two roles that can't really be done by part-timers but they're few and far between. Besides, the systems ensure that each process we undertake has a natural flow to it."

"What do you mean?"

"Well, I've talked about the different roles within the office but there are also lots of processes."

"Such as?"

"Well, a potential client walking in the door for example. Someone walks in off the street saying that they need a new accountant. The responsibility for speaking to that person is with the office receptionist; that's Victoria. She knows to take a few details about the client, what sort of business they have etc and then make a decision about who is the most appropriate Principal Adviser to deal with them."

"What's a Principal Adviser?"

"Oh it's just the name we came up for the role that has overall responsibility for a group of clients. We've got three Principal advisers; Me, Akram and Rebecca who I think you met this morning. We're the three most experienced accountants here and every client is assigned to one of us as

Chapter 23

Principal Advisers. We are also responsible for bringing in new clients."

"Unless you're not available in which case, someone else deputises."

"It sounds like you've been here for years! But you're right. I'm sure you've guessed that we have a system for seeing new clients. We all sat down and talked about it one day. The three of us had different techniques that we found worked but sometimes found that we didn't get the client. We pooled our ideas, got a few others from courses and books and came up with a way of running a potential client meeting that got the best results."

"You've got a lot of clients for just three of you."

"We have but again the systems kick in. Once we've signed up the new client, we have to complete an email that goes to the client data administrator, that's Elizabeth by the way, telling them about the new client."

"I don't think I've met Elizabeth." said Ruby mentally walking her way around the office and trying to picture everyone."

"You won't have done", responded Matt. "That's because she works in South Africa. We have a little team out there who do various support tasks for us. Liz looks after the database and all sorts of client care issues. She has a long list of things that she has to do once she gets that email."

'Oh wow, South Africa' thought Ruby wondering if there might be a chance of all expenses paid trip one day but thinking better of asking. "What sort of things does she do?"

"Well," replied Matt, "we found that so many things that can go wrong can be avoided by getting the setup process right. If all the correct information is put onto the database and the client completes all the documents that we need at the start, then 101 things that could potentially go wrong on that client's affairs over the next few years, won't."

Chapter 23

"But how does that reduce the work for you?"

"Well, whenever something goes wrong, it's the Principal Adviser that gets dragged in to sort it out. I know that Chas and Ron and even Eric spent quite a bit of their time dealing with trivial problems that could have been avoided. It used to be like that with me. I'd come back from a meeting and there would be ten phone calls to return, only one of which was actually a client needing some advice. The others were all things that could be avoided."

"What, all problems?"

"No, some of them were clients that didn't understand a letter or email that we sent them. And many of these letters and emails were about standard things. So, we produced standard templates about every single thing we could think of; you can access them all through your systems. If someone rang us up because they didn't understand something, then we recognised that the template wasn't good enough and we re-wrote it."

"And everything ran smoothly as a result?"

"Yes, but it wasn't an overnight process. There was a stage when I thought that we'd wasted all our time doing the systems. We had all these systems, but we were still getting loads of things going wrong. I spoke to Ron about it, although he'd been retired for years by then and he said it was just growing pains, but I wasn't convinced."

"Why?"

"Because growing pains implied that the problem was simply that the staff weren't experienced enough and that it was all down to people. I felt that it was more than that. I felt that the systems weren't good enough. And then I realised what the problem was."

Ruby looked blankly at him.

Chapter 23

"Well, each of the systems were fine in themselves but they didn't flow. Once we cracked that one, we really started to reap the benefits of all the work we put in. Let me show you the process that a set of accounts goes through including the bits that you'll be involved in, and it will all make more sense."

Chapter 24

The man in the bowler hat

Every now and again I find myself talking to one or two people about Kaizen.

My firm's success has always depended on our collective ability to constantly improve what we do and how we do it. The Japanese call this 'Kaizen' – constant improvement. The word translates to mean change (kai) for the good (zen).

Businesses that follow that Kaizen approach believe that everything can always be improved.

Practitioners of Kaizen believe that we all need to have an open 'growth mindset' for Kaizen to be present so that there is never a period of status quo. There must be continuous effort to improve; these can be small changes over time, which in the long term add up to larger change, or these can be one-off changes. When this doesn't happen, technology, competitors and client expectations overtake us.

Even worse, some of the things that we had right in the past start to go wrong. How often do you find yourself having to get involved in sorting

Chapter 24

out problems that you know you fixed many years ago? Then you find out that for many months that particular process has been operated without following the systems which served you well in the past. Infuriating, isn't it?

The Kaizen approach was at the heart of the Toyota Production system which revolutionised the car manufacturing industry and has influenced many production processes throughout the world. Embracing Kaizen means that despite challenges or difficulties, your organisation believes that you can work out a solution by:

- Responding positively to any issues,
- Learning new skills,
- Improving existing skills,
- Build new insights and
- Master a better way for your company.

A lot of this sounds like complicated theory but I guarantee that it's at the heart of most of what you will find yourself dealing with this week.

When we started our systems journey all those years ago, I had a wise older lady called Betty who worked for me. Whilst a few of her younger colleagues were resisting my attempts to bring order to their chaos, Betty said something really interesting to me.

"None of this is new though. Back in the sixties we always had the man in the bowler hat walking round with his clipboard."

'Of course,' I thought. The Time and Motion Man.

The concept of 'time and motion' for highly fashionable in business once upon a time. It combined the techniques of time study (how long things should take basically) with motion study which was a technique for improving work methods. Everyone who worked in a factory (and a significant percentage of the working population did in those days) was familiar with the time and motion man.

Chapter 24

Whilst it all seems so old-fashioned now, any business needs to use this method or something similar if it is to evolve into an operation which is not dependent on its owner and still remain profitable.

In fact, as you reduce the dependency of the business on your skills, knowledge and working hours, the last job you should relinquish is that of the man in the bowler hat.

In chapter 18, I described how you write systems. Each task that you do has a system. Put them all together and you have a process.

And that's where you need to find your bowler hat because whilst each system may be correct in itself, that doesn't mean that the process will work. And it definitely doesn't mean that it will be efficient.

To ensure that your processes will work, you have to conduct a walk-through test.

There are hundreds of walk-through tests you could undertake, and it might take you many months (or even years) to walk through all the processes that exist. Your time is precious, so you must pick one where fixing it will create the biggest benefit.

The benefit might come from fixing a problem that is costing you lots of money. Or it might be unfulfilled potential.

Either way, the way you undertake a walk-through process is as following:

1. Get yourself in the mindset of those who are following the process.

2. There is lots of information that you have which you think is common sense but is only common-sense to someone with your experience. Don't skip the detail

3. Find a context.

Chapter 24

4. This is important you need to think about what really happens. Not the theory but the reality. Imagine a scenario as you walk through the process. A new customer making an order, a decision to recruit a new member of staff. A situation that is relevant to this process.

5. Find where it all begins.

6. This may be much earlier than you think. An order from a customer doesn't begin when they place the order, it begins when they first make contact with your sales department. Do you get the correct information about them at that stage? Do you capture it correctly in your Customer Relationship Manager (CRM) system? Systems can be simplified if the systems before them have done some of the heavy lifting.

7. Read through the first system and ensure that all the steps are listed (as numbers) and the way that each step is done is explained (in letters in between).

8. Consider issues where information needs to be entered into software packages e.g. databases, accounts systems, payroll software, CRM packages. Detail exactly what data needs to be entered and where.

9. Consider if the way each step and each system is conducted completes the task in the optimum time.

10. As you reach the end consider how the process moves on from this system to the next system. Issues to consider:

    a. Is the next system (i.e. the next part of the process) conducted by the same person?

    b. If the next system is conducted by a different person? If so, consider how they will be notified that they need to undertake the next system. This could be automated via the software you are using, or it could be a push notification via email, WhatsApp etc or maybe a simple call.

c. Do multiple people need to be notified to start several different systems? For example, completion of new staff paperwork might be followed by notification to the staff member's new team leader, the IT department to set up the logon and hardware, payroll department etc.

11. Move onto the next system and repeat points 7 to 9.

12. If you identify issues that could be improved by amending an earlier system, return to that earlier system and make such amendments. Re-trace your steps back to the later system. You may need to do this multiple times.

13. Consider situations where systems branch e.g. as per the example in 10c above. This may require you to walk in a few different directions. Do these branches each have their own endings? Or do they rejoin later on when each path taken brings you back to the same point?

14. When you have reached of the process or perhaps as far as you feel you need to go e.g. the raising of an invoice to a customer, stop and assess whether your entire process achieves the goal you set out for it. If not, re-visit, re-visit, re-visit until it does.

The man in the bowler hat with his clipboard would have done all the above in a physical sense. Walking round a factory assessing the production line.

Your walk-throughs will be an assessment of both physical and digital. Much of the exercise can be done on your laptop or PC. But depending on what your business does, sometimes you will need to physically visit the place where the work is done. Do your systems work in practice as well as theory? Talk to those who do the work. Find out the practical difficulties with the system you have produced.

And that's it. Do this over and over and you will be practitioner of Kaizen. Well, the 'less dependent' version of it anyway.

Chapter 25

Good arguments and bad arguments

Joe and Dan were arguing again.

They'd spent much of their life arguing. "Why are you wearing the same clothes as me?" and "the ball definitely crossed the line" were replaced with "why aren't you looking after this customer?" and "you need to manage your team better."

They'd pretty much argued about everything over the years.

In the business, there was usually only one winner. Joe would get louder when he didn't feel his opinion was being listened to. Dan would get embarrassed and go silent.

But the strategic planning sessions with Matt seemed to have matured their relationship.

Joe had been negative about most of the issues they discussed initially. He was always ready to blame someone. Staff members, his brother, the economy, customers and occasionally even his father.

Chapter 25

But Matt had persisted in trying to bring the issues back to the people in the room. "Yes, but hypothetically if we agree that the staff are all "rubbish", what are you going to do so that they aren't 'rubbish'?". That sort of thing.

And that's where Dan stepped in with well-observed suggestions.

Truth be known, he had never worked as hard as Joe. He might like to pretend he did but often he was answering inconsequent emails or "managing" contracts which were actually being managed by someone else.

The lads on site liked Dan. His visits were often a morale booster because he'd ask about their families or chat about the weekend's football results. He knew them as people not just as workers.

But when they were up against a deadline, Dan's presence was a nuisance as it stopped them getting the work done. This was especially the case on bigger jobs. Because of the impact on cash flow, David wouldn't be able to stop himself getting involved at the slightest hint of a problem. He'd be on site asking questions, demanding answers, side-lining his youngest son and sometimes doing more damage than good.

No-one was brave enough to tell David that some of the delays were caused by Dan. David was never aware that some of the good staff who had left over the years had done so because they'd been given the blame.

Dan had pretty much coasted his way through his career so far. But the staffing crisis and the strategic planning sessions had given Dan a better understanding of the business and he loved it. He loved the numbers, he loved the plans, he loved the debates about strategy.

Dan was now in charge of most of the office functions. Although he was no bookkeeper, he knew his way round the reports on the Cloud system and looked at the important ones most days. Shona had taught Dan most of the basics of cash flow management and he'd brought in a really

Chapter 25

good part-time credit controller who he spoke to in two scheduled meetings a week.

He'd also spent some money upgrading the IT system and setting up some protocols for everyone to follow so all customer documentation was easily accessible.

Joe meanwhile, had become a better manager. Matt had spent a little bit of time teaching him a few management techniques.

The first one was pretty simple. Just to notice the things that were going right not just those that were going wrong.

Like most people do, Joe judged everyone by his own standards. A thief always assumes that other people are trying to steal from them. A really honest person always assumes that other people will be honest.

Joe worked hard so he just assumed everyone else should too. When they did, he just treated it as what was expected from them. No-one ever got a pat on the back, literal or metaphorical.

But lately, he'd made an effort to say thank you for jobs completed well. He questioned why he'd found it so hard to start with but now it was becoming second nature.

And Matt had given him a different way to tackle staff who weren't quite coming up to standard. He'd find something positive to say about their work first, then tackle the thing that wasn't so good and finished with a positive comment about how confident he was that the work would be better next time. The classic proverbial 'shit sandwich'.

Whilst 'the lads' were a little nervous initially about this new Joe, they were responding well. Staff were asking his advice about problems then going away and dealing with the problem themselves. Not all the time of course. Not everyone steps up, but Joe was noticing those that did.

Chapter 25

In their two different ways, Joe and Dan were starting to think that perhaps the business could work without David after all.

Most of all, they were starting to see each other as business partners.

Their arguments had turned into good arguments. Discussions around late payments of invoices from customers weren't about blame but about solutions. Dan respected Joe's knowledge of the products and the customers. Joe respected Dan's knowledge about Health and Safety and legal matters. They also worked out a neat 'good cop/bad cop' routine for dealing with problems. No surprise about who was who in each situation.

Whilst they weren't leaning on David so much, he was still around but his presence meant they knew they had to get on. What would happen if it was just them?

Chapter 26

Leading from the back

Angela Merkel was Chancellor of Germany from 22nd November 2005 to 8th December 2021. 16 years and 18 days. That's an extraordinary length of time for a democratically elected leader to stay in power. Unless you decide the result of the elections yourself, like Vladimir Putin.

But it occurred to me that if Merkel were British, she would never have become Prime Minister.

Maybe foreign secretary or perhaps minister for transport. That's if she even got selected as an MP in the first place.

That's because the British and German expectations of leadership are so vastly different. Is that because our cultures are different, or is it down to our different voting systems (Germany has proportional representation whilst we operate a first past the post system)? Or is it because the German people realised many decades ago, that charismatic strong leaders had more downsides than ups? Let's not go there on that one.

Chapter 26

Whatever the reasons, the fact that the two most successful economies in Europe have such vastly different expectations and requirements from their leaders, demonstrates that there are lots of different ways to lead.

When the pandemic hit, in almost every country in the world, there was a "we're all in this together" spirit. We'd found a common enemy (a virus only visible through a powerful microscope) and we all pulled together.

Well for a few weeks anyway.

Steve Backley, one of my co-writers in Accidental Millionaires, predicted that would happen well before it did.

He called it "week 4 syndrome". Up to that point, everyone tends to pull together but week 4 is when the cracks start to show. I thought it was noticeable that the first protests about lockdown started in various parts of the world in week 4 just as my friend Mystic Steve predicted!

This was human nature at work and what happened on a global scale is what would probably happen at your business if something bad were to happen to you and you were incapacitated (or worse). There would probably be four stages:

Survival phase when everyone acts on instinct and (mostly) in a very selfless way

A "New normal" phase as everyone gets used to the new situation

A realisation stage where everyone starts to understand the contribution you made to the business. Shame you weren't around to see it!

A downturn in results combined with everyone looking after themselves and a loss of collective identity

This doomsday scenario should give you two things to think about in terms of your leadership style:

Chapter 26

Have you created a set of guiding principles and behaviours that will sustain the business in your absence? Maybe something which at the absolute worst will stretch out the time-frame between stages 1 and 4 above?

Have you put something in place so that a leader will be found or is ready to step in?

If the latter, then it's quite possible that there might be the emergence of a new leader who is as good as or maybe even better than you were.

The difference between a successful business owner and a not so successful one is that the successful ones are much better at catastrophising. This usually happens around 4am in the morning after a particular problem has arisen the previous day and goes something like this:

"If that's gone wrong, how many others have gone wrong?"

"If loads have gone wrong, we are going to lose all our best customers and get sued"

"We won't have enough for the overheads and my drawings"

"I'm going to lose my house"

"My life is over"

By 6am, rational thought has returned, and you have a plan for fixing whatever it is that has gone wrong. By 9.05am, members of your team will be aware of that plan. The more conscientious ones will get it and support the solutions. Some will roll their eyes behind your back questioning to themselves what all the fuss is about.

But you and I know that the secret to a successful business over a long period of time is the combination of all that catastrophising. As one of my clients once said to me "the secret to our success is that when there's

Chapter 26

a problem, we are ALL over it".

We also know that without you, there would have been no catastrophising and the problem would have been ignored. Whilst the implications would not have been as disastrous as the 4am version of you thought they would be, the impact on the business would be a negative one. Add all those occasions together and you have the difference between a successful business and an unsuccessful one.

That's what being a leader is all about.

In the book From Good To Great by Jim Collins, their research identified 11 companies who had outperformed the market by at least 6 times every year for 15 years.

Collins' team identified that the 11 companies all had what they called a Level 5 executive; one who builds enduring greatness through a paradoxical blend of personal humility and professional will.

So, what can we learn from level 5 leaders that will help you making your business less dependent on you?

In addition to personal humility, Collins' team identified four key issues:

Create super results, a clear catalyst in the transition from good to great

Demonstrates an unwavering resolve to do whatever must be done to produce the best long-term results no matter how difficult

Sets the standard of building and enduring great company will settle for nothing less

Looks in the mirror not out the window to apportion responsibility for poor results never blaming other people external factors or bad luck

But that sounds very much like you will need to be involved in a hands-on way. If you want your business less dependent on you, then you will

Chapter 26

no longer be able to lead from the front. You are going to need to lead from the back. will need to do the following:

Build an exceptional reporting system that enables everyone to see the impact of their individual or team performance supported by a dynamic finance department that not only reports on the figures but investigates them and acts on the findings

Create and inspire a small group of senior managers who understand the critical nature of acting on any problems they find

Find a way of communicating with the wider team to continually educate them on the standards that the company aspires to

Teach your team the difference between internal and external attribution and how they work with staff beneath them

Of course, you must match your strategies in this regard to your personality.

Many business owners spend far too much time in conflict with difficult members of staff. What I would call those with a win-lose mindset, who believe they can only win in their relationship with you if you lose.

You might change the mindset of those people but it's unlikely.

It's better to have them surrounded by those who share your values. And then find ways to keep them motivated. There are a few ways of doing this:

Churchillian-like speeches. If that's your thing

Regular provision of information explaining reasons behind doing things in certain ways

Cold hard cash earnt via results-based bonuses. This is harder than it sounds, and every bonus scheme has its flaws. There are two dangers

Chapter 26

being that the bonus scheme is not rewarding enough to motivate anyone or that employees work the system to maximise their bonuses but not for the benefit of the firm

An "if you can measure it, you can manage it" approach where you measure performance on every job and interrogate the reasons being any under-performing situation

Whatever your methods for leading are, keep doing them. Whilst your business doesn't need Angela Merkel to lead it, it definitely needs you. Even if you're in the background.

Chapter 27

Some me time

"I just need a bit of ME time" David said to Matt who nodded like he'd heard the line a few hundred times before. Which he had.

"I thought things were going really well" replied Matt.

"Oh they are, they are" said David proudly as he thought about the huge leaps his two sons had made. "The office is running smoother, there's less friction between the staff and the customers are happier. I haven't had anyone shout at me in months," chuckled the founder and majority shareholder of Bright Interiors ltd.

"And do you know what? I'm actually really enjoying it now."

Matt nodded, knowing what David was about to say.

"But I'm not getting any younger, am I? And I've got a few things I'd really like to spend a bit more time on. Jean and I have got lots of ideas about days out that we could take the grandchildren on. And we'd like to have a few holidays a year."

Chapter 27

"Anything else?" prodded Matt.

"Yep, loads. A few away day football matches, meet up with my friends for a beer a bit more often, that sort of thing. And maybe you and I could get out for another game of golf some time without me having to zoom off."

Matt winced at the memory of the last time they'd played three or four years earlier. David had taken a call around the 8th hole, had barked instructions to someone whilst walking down the fairway and then four or five holes later had apologised profusely and abruptly headed off the clubhouse to sort out whatever problem had occurred.

"So, I'd hoped all the changes would be reducing some of the impact on you. Why isn't that happening?" enquired Matt.

David smiled a philosophical smile.

"Ok, so there are two flaws in the plan from a personal point of view. From everyone else's point of view, it's perfect. But what I hadn't reckoned on was that we would get more work. Lots of extra bits on some of the jobs we're doing because we're more proactive, quotes on other work in different areas from existing customers and quite a few new clients as well."

"Bugger" said Matt smiling. "So, you're getting drawn back into overseeing some of the contracts?"

"Yep."

"Why don't you see if Phil would come back? Ruby doesn't think he's committed to the place he's gone to work at."

"I've thought of that", said David "but it would cause uproar. Joe and Phil had a real ding-dong when Phil said he was going."

Matt decided not to push the point and tilted his head in a way that

Chapter 27

indicated that maybe that wasn't terminal.

"Anyway, how's that daughter of mine getting on?" asked David changing the subject.

"Pretty good" replied Matt. "She's like a little sponge. From what I've seen and what I've been told, she doesn't need to be taught anything twice".

Matt paused. "You're not thinking of poaching her to come and work for the family firm, are you?"

David chuckled. "Don't worry Matt, I'm not sure Bright Interiors could handle Joe and Ruby in the same company. You should have heard the arguments the first time she beat him at pool! They didn't speak for two weeks. Besides, I think a career in your world suits her skills better".

"Good" replied Matt. "Now I want to run through some management changes that I think will help you get a bit more me time.

Meanwhile in an office on the floor above, Ruby was using the opportunity of an afternoon helping Akram to pick his brains.

"Don't take this the wrong way; because I've seen how not having systems really made life difficult for Dad when he was running his business, but do you find that some of the staff don't really like following your systems?"

"Well first of all, they're not my systems Ruby, they're ours because almost everyone here has contributed to their content in one way or another. But you have a point. One or two people have objected over the years." Matt smiled.

"Why are you smiling?"

"Well, there are some people in life that just seem to enjoy chaos and just can't or won't work in an organised way. Free spirits they called

Chapter 27

themselves. The 'members of staff most likely to get us sued' is what I call them. I had a couple of run-ins in the early days with two people who shall remain anonymous but most people like working in a structured way. It's a lot less hassle."

"Doesn't it get a bit boring sometimes?"

"Now that's the mistake that a lot of people make. They think that because you have a standard way of doing everything that you're going to become some kind of robot when in fact the opposite is true. The fact is that there are thousands of things every day that you can't systemise. Even if you create standard agendas for phone calls and meetings, you can't systemise those actual calls or meetings because they're with human beings.

What we've done is systemise everything else so that you've got far more energy to deal with all the things that you can't systemise. And instead of learning to be a bean-counter, you're learning to be someone who can really make a difference to your clients."

"OK. I can see that"

"You see, those staff that don't get organised actually spend less time dealing with their clients than those that are organised. They find themselves with a huge volume of work that only they can deal with and then they don't take enough time with the people they come into contact with. And when they do come into contact with those people, sometimes they are flustered and struggling to provide the right advice because there is no system to make it easy for them."

Matt looked at Ruby and asked if that made sense. Ruby nodded.

"You see Ruby, when you have systems, you're not turning people into machines, you're giving them a really good machine to run. And the truth is we all love using good machines, whether it's the latest gadget for the home or a really fast car."

Chapter 27

"I see that. And apart from the two anonymous individuals that's pretty much how everyone else sees it?"

"Pretty much, although there have been one or two others over the years who like the way that the systems make their life easier but don't meet their side of the bargain. They're the ones who always cut corners when they follow the systems. Of course, they never cut corners if doing so would make their life more difficult. They do it on the bits of the system that affect other people and all sorts of things go wrong because Vicky hasn't had the email to remind her to do whatever or Akram needs to know a particular piece of information, but it's never been put onto the database."

"You make them sound quite selfish."

"Exactly. We're all part of a team and we all have to play our part. Anything else is selfish. We all rely on each other."

"That's what Shona told me. She said she likes feeling that she's part of a team and she said that wasn't the case at her previous firm"

"Did she tell you who her previous firm was?"

"No, who was it?"

"She worked for Chas at Mortimore's. She was there when I was there actually, but she was relatively junior back in those days. Then, a couple of years ago she rang me up because she knew we were looking for staff and wanted to join us."

"That explains your comment earlier"

"It does, but I actually tried to talk her into staying with Chas. When she first rang me, we had a long chat about why she was unhappy there and I told her what I thought she should do but a few weeks later she rang me and said she'd handed her notice in anyway and if we didn't give her a job someone else would. I rang Chas up and explained that if

Chapter 27

she was leaving anyway, she might as well come and work for us but I'm sure he still thinks that we poached her."

"And that's why he stopped talking to you?"

"Maybe. But I think he was just looking for an excuse. I think I was a reminder of how much stress he was under!"

"Why did she hate working there so much?"

"Well, Shona's really organised and even though they don't have documented systems like us, she always had her own system. Chas took on a new manager called James and although he's a clever guy he's always making life difficult for everyone that works there."

"How do you mean?"

"Well, Shona told me that she always planned her workload. She'd book up audits and work out which of the juniors would go with her and then the day she was due to go out to the client, James would say he needed that junior for another job, and she'd have to go on her own. Then the job would take twice as long so she wouldn't get back to the office in time to get the other jobs she had done and so on. She just didn't feel in control there."

"But if she liked being in control of everything, surely your systems took control away from her?

"No, not at all. Everyone has control of their own workload here as long as they work within the systems that we've all agreed. And besides, Shona brought in loads of ideas when she joined, which is exactly what we want everyone to do."

There was a pause before Matt spoke again.

"OK. Got your head round it all? Ready to start work tomorrow?"

Chapter 27

"I don't think I'll remember everything." Ruby replied.

"I'm sure you won't but I think you've got a pretty good head start. Besides, if you're not sure about anything you've got the systems to refer to or more likely someone will hold your hand as you get used to the way we do things around here."

"OK. Great see you tomorrow"

As Ruby drove away from her first day at the office so many ideas were going round her head. The work she was going to be doing, what she could tell Dad about the place but most of all the opportunities that it seemed to hold for her.

Chapter 28

Succession

Despite its extravagant storylines, larger-than-life characters and award-winning acting, the hit HBO series, Succession, shed a light on the real-life implications of poor business succession planning.

The blunt and often profane Logan Roy takes centre stage as the protagonist. The show delves into the power struggles within the wealthy Roy family as they vie for control of the family business, both before and after Logan's eventual demise. Despite Logan's straightforward demeanour, he fails to engage in effective communication or succession planning with his children and company.

This lack of preparation is not unique to the Roy family. A survey conducted by PwC in 2021 revealed that only around one-third of family-owned businesses have a succession plan in place. This leaves a significant portion of such businesses vulnerable to the kind of dramatic conflicts seen on the show.

When I was in the early stages of my career, I had a client who died whilst in bed with his mistress (I was told that bit in confidence later). At the peak of his earning power, the business was completely dependent on him.

Chapter 28

I was asked to come to a meeting at their offices. As was usual in those days, I under-estimated the time to get there and arrived ten minutes late. As I walked in, I met his wife, two adult children, major customer who was a personal friend of his, lawyer and assistant, secretary and two most senior members of his team.

They were all waiting for me. Not because I was the only one not there. But because they were waiting for me to advise what to do. No-one else knew where to begin.

Most of the business was in his head. There were two major jobs underway that appeared to have no paperwork.

The best we could do was to do a deal with a competitor to take the company on at their own risk. We got some money for the family, but it could have been so much more.

You're a business owner and one day, I'm sure you want to either sell your business or pass it on to future generations. Here are my 3 lessons you can learn from Succession in your own business.

Lesson 1: Don't lead alone – be a bit more like a Ronald (See Chapter 5).
If you've got this bit right, the biggest challenge of succession will be deciding who steps into your shoes. Oh, and placating those who thought it would be them!

If you're an Elton, there probably is no succession.

But that doesn't mean your business has no value though. You have a list of customers, a contact book and maybe some products and intellectual property.

You have three choices:
Train up one of your staff as best you can, to take over. Assuming you aren't actually the real Elton, this is possible. The apprentice who has worked as your assistant for years might be ready. They might not be as

Chapter 28

good as you, but they'll know the customers even if you might need to be on the end of a phone occasionally.

Find a small competitor who is ambitious. This might be their chance to merge your business with theirs and take a big step forward.

Find a bigger competitor who can absorb your customer base into theirs.

The likelihood is that the deal in 1 and 2 above will need you to agree to accept payments over a long period of time. The third might be harder to find and risks alerting your customers and staff to your intention to retire.

In Succession, Logan Roy is the key to Waystar Royco's success. His tenacity, business savvy, and strategic vision have propelled the company forward. He understands the business and his audience like no one else. As he puts it:

"I make my nut off what people really want. Don't tell me about people—I'd go flat broke in a week if I didn't."

Logan's belief that he can do everything better than anyone else, has made him indispensable to the business. When he suffers a stroke in season 1, Waystar Royco's stock price plummets, triggering a chain of events that nearly ruins the company. Logan is Waystar. While he has appointed key people and advisors, he cannot relinquish control of the firm which has real negative consequences.

As a business owner, you must remember that while you are intrinsically linked to the success of the business, you are not solely responsible for it. Surrounding yourself with capable and dedicated individuals who share the same vision and are willing to make sacrifices is crucial for sustainable long-term success.

Lesson 2: Start succession planning early
Recent research indicates that only 35% of businesses have a formal succession planning process for critical roles, and 58% of family businesses in the UK have no succession plan at all.

Chapter 28

In Succession, we have Kendall, vulnerable and insecure, yearning for his father's validation. Shiv, despite her sharp intellect, often feels side-lined for being a woman in a patriarchal world. And then there's Roman, whose life is plagued by a multitude of personal issues.

The problem is each of them feels entitled to the role due to promises made by their father, whose leadership style involves testing rather than nurturing his successors. This lack of consistency and preparation leads to chaos and conflict within the family.

The fact that a business as significant as Waystar Royco, valued at approximately $80 billion, has no formal succession plan in place is evidence of short-sightedness. With an aging CEO and no clear successor, the company is susceptible to instability and internal strife. When the CEO unexpectedly passes away in season 4, the emotionally stunted siblings engage in a game of manipulation and deceit to claim the coveted position.

It is crucial for businesses, regardless of size, to anticipate and plan for the departure of key personnel. Whether it is due to retirement, career changes, illness, or unfortunate events, having a solid succession plan is essential. Here are some proactive steps to take:

Assess the impact of the absence of key personnel in critical areas of the business.

Regularly identify potential candidates for internal hiring and succession.

Look beyond seniority and consider young prospects who possess the necessary skills and potential.

Communicate to potential successors that their career progression could lead to key roles in the future, encouraging them to take on additional responsibilities and prepare for the role.

Determine any necessary training and development programs for prospective successors.

Chapter 28

In cases of planned departures, allowing the prospective successor to shadow the departing individual during a prolonged handover process can provide valuable experience and knowledge transfer.

By starting succession planning early and committing to it, businesses can ensure continuity, stability, and a smooth transition when key personnel depart. Succession planning is not just a strategic decision; it is a crucial aspect of long-term business sustainability.

Lesson 3: Be a family
Humiliating employees through demeaning tactics like "Boar on the floor" (Succession season 2, episode 3) may provide temporary entertainment, but it does not bring out the best in them. Fostering a culture that encourages employees to thrive is essential.

Whilst investing in the learning and development of employees at all levels of the company is crucial, this sometimes means you don't spend enough time mentoring those at the upper levels. This can manifest itself into a situation where the buck stops with you but your number two feels that they are making an equal contribution to the success of the company whilst remaining blissfully unaware (or deliberately ignorant) of the challenges you address every week which are often outside their comfort zone.

If you've worked with your senior team for many years, you might be more like a family than a business already. Hopefully one which is not as dysfunctional as the Roy family.

But such relationships can be so settled that owners are frightened of upsetting the apple cart and talking about the future. "Retirement" becomes the elephant in the room that no-one dares mention. Meanwhile, the senior employee may be making some assumptions about what the future holds.

At the time of writing, there is a huge amount of money being invested via private equity in the professional services world. Big accountancy, lawyers, surveyors' practices are springing up purely as a result of mergers and acquisitions.

Chapter 28

But the collateral damage from these consolidations are the ambitions of those "number twos". The young men and women with middle-age on the horizon who have worked loyally for "the firm" for many years and suddenly realise that instead of taking over one day, they are now a small cog in a big wheel.

It's quite possible of course that the previous owner of those businesses simply wanted to maximise the amount they generated for their retirement. Maybe that's your over-riding priority, too.

I know that there is always a little bit of sadness that something they spent most of their career building, simply gets swallowed up into something much bigger. And that the relationship between the owner and the person who they worked with most closely, is often damaged beyond repair.

There are alternatives but as mentioned in lesson 2, the discussions need to start early.

In many businesses, we have helped put together a "Passport to Partnership" document. This sets out the history of the business, the challenges it has overcome, the risks the founder and current owner took in the past, the hours they put in to building its intangible assets (customers base, products, intellectual property, systems and processes) and the alternative exit strategies for the owner. The intention is to share this document with the senior members of the team with whom you might negotiate some kind of deal for them to take over.

The document should end with a simple message at the end that the owner would like to sit down and discuss a variety of strategies with the company's accountant (it's always handy to get us along as we can be bad cop if required and diffuse any misunderstandings or disagreements.

This gets the discussion up and running.

For all we know, the "number two" may have no interest at all in running the place. They might prefer to help the owner find a buyer and become an

Chapter 28

employee with the new owners. Cue a little deal where you offer them a bonus to help get the sale through.

Or they might have a rich uncle who will help them buy it. Or be prepared to do an earnt-out arrangement over a number of years. Or perhaps they might prefer a partial buyout where you are retained as a consultant and sleeping partner.

There are lots of ways such a deal could be structured. Some might require a holding company to be created, or a share option scheme. Other deals might be better constructed via a Limited Liability Partnership.

The point is that it's a journey and with the right advisers hopefully you can get to a destination that appeals to everyone.

And if not, well there's always the sale to a third party to fall back on.

The final alternative to all the above would be to "do a Logan Roy" and string various people along for years allowing them to believe that they are the chosen one. Then die on your private jet before the decision is ever made.

I suspect Logan Roy would have enjoyed looking down on the chaos that ensued. You can do that if you're a billionaire.

But if there is no private jet, then it might be decision time.

Chapter 29

Reaching the promised land

Jean was concerned.

Despite all the positive discussions around the business and the improved relationship between her two sons, her husband David seemed to be busier than ever.

He was travelling around far more than he had been previously. When he wasn't, he seemed to be spending a lot more time in his office at home. Questions about why he was so busy always seemed to get the same reply; "I'm working on my masterplan" he'd say with a glint in his eye.

But it was a glint she hadn't seen for many years. It was the same glint when he signed up a contract to fit out 25 offices in London over a two-year period.

But that was 20 years ago.

"Come on then" she said. "What are you up to?"

Chapter 29

"Right" replied David, "I need your advice."

David ran through what he was thinking of doing and Jean listened. She liked the goal, which was basically a comfortable retirement, and with her children looked after financially, and a few hours of consultancy work for David.

"Well?" said David when the overwhelmingly enthusiastic reaction he was hoping for, didn't arrive.

Jean looked out into the garden.

"I think there's a bit of a flaw".

David looked at Jean trying to work out what the flaw was. He'd spent hours going through everything he did in the business. He'd listed out all the areas where he was worried about his experience being missed. He'd structured the training sessions he was going to run and the reporting he was going to insist was done on a monthly basis.

He'd documented the key roles in the business including what Joe and Dan would be responsible for. He'd even written out flow charts of the critical processes and produced checklists for some of the key tasks.

"Well?" he pleaded to his wife of twenty-five years.

"It's the sales side of things," said Jean.

"You've always talked about the importance of knowing your product and believing in it. Now you're just going to employ someone you don't know to do that part of the work."

"Hmmm" mumbled David.

"They won't have your passion. They'll turn up for an interview, you'll take on the one who gives the best chat and then 6 months down the line they'll be off to another company who is paying slightly better money.

Chapter 29

Possibly taking some of our customers with them!"

David had to admit she had a point. "Well, what if Joe and Dan share the responsibility for sales?" he said possibly grasping at straws. "I used to do all those jobs."

"Yes, but the company was much smaller then and you'd built it up from scratch. Joe and Dan have a lot to deal with and let's face it they need to modernise a lot of things as well."

David bristled at the suggestion that perhaps he'd allowed his life's work to become a little bit dated but again he thought better of protesting.

"So, what's the answer then?" he said.

"You know what the answer is dear" said his wife in a slightly more patronising tone than he was completely happy with. "But that would require you to swallow your pride, won't it?"

Indeed, it would. But if David was to reach the promised land of a comfortable retirement, then it had to be done.

The next six weeks flew by.

Dan had organised a joint venture with one of their major suppliers. An innovative new heat pump system they would be installing in most of their office re-fits. Environmentally and local-press friendly. Plenty of content for their Instagram account.

The day of the launch arrived.

Trevor wasn't used to being this smart during a workday. But he loved it that he got invited to this sort of event.

He might be in semi-retirement, but he thought of himself as part of the fabric of Bright Interiors and appreciated it that clearly David and the

Chapter 29

boys (having known them since childhood, they would always be "the boys" to him) thought so too.

He was one of the first to arrive. He looked quizzically at the young lady offering him a drink. "Do I know you?" he said.

"I'm Madison" she said, "Billy's daughter".

"Good grief" said Trevor, "I remember when you were born", also remembering all the extra work he had to do after his young colleague Billy rushed off site when he got the call that Madison's Mum had gone into labour three weeks early.

The offices and warehouse were as smart and as clean as they had ever been in the history of Bright Interiors.

There were tables with tea and coffee on, another with lots of champagne bottles. Various people were shown into the Bright Interiors warehouse / event venue for the day, by more young people who seemed to bear a passing resemblance to other members of Bright Interiors staff. "Typical David" thought Trevor "keeping it in the family".

Trevor recognised about half of the people filing in. Customers, suppliers, Matt Pevy the company accountant, Ruby Bright but also lots of younger businessmen and businesswomen he didn't. But there was one face he hadn't expected to see there. A face that hadn't seen him yet.

Trevor arced round the room like a spy on a mission and sidled up to the tall chap he'd trained when he first left school.

"You're the last person I expected to see here" he said.

Slightly startled but with a smile on his face, Phil Morrison turned to face his old mentor.

"Trev" Phil said gleefully, "I was really hoping you'd be here".

Chapter 29

"Well, I still work here, sort of" replied Trevor "but you don't".

"Ah well Trevor, it's all water under the bridge. I'm pleased the old firm is doing so well. And you never know, I might need my old job back one day" sighed Phil in a way that made Trevor think he wasn't quite being told the truth.

But before he could ask any questions, another young face appeared.

"Phil, you're needed" said Ruby nodding her head towards the front of the room.

"Sorry, Trev," apologised Phil, "duty calls"

Ruby suddenly realised who the old chap with the puzzled expression was. "Uncle Trev!" she exclaimed hugging the man she remembered as the one who entertained her with silly jokes and let her win at cards at the family New Year's Eve parties all those years ago.

But before they could reminisce, a booming voice asked for their attention. "Dan and I have got a few things to say" called Joe.

Dan spoke from the heart about the journey the firm had been on and how he'd not always been its most reliable employee which got a few wry smiles. Joe looked at his notes and thanked the supplier that they were teaming up with and the opportunities it would bring. Then the Product Manager from the supply company waffled on for far too long about technical details that went way over the head of 90% of the room.

In one particularly long pause, Dan jumped in to save proceedings and announced that his father wanted to say a few words as well.

David tried not to make eye contact with the room. As energetic and effusive as he had been throughout his business career, speaking in front of a big room of people was way outside his comfort zone. And he felt a little emotional about it as well.

Chapter 29

"I've got another announcement to make" he said to the hushed room.

Pause.

"I'm not retiring!" he exclaimed.

For some reason, this announcement didn't get the laugh he was hoping for, so he carried on anyway.

"But I am taking a step back. As of tomorrow, Joe is going to be Managing Director and Dan will be Operations and Finance Director."

After a smattering of applause, David continued, "and I'd like to announce the appointment of Phil Morrison as our new sales director." Cue another little round of applause as Phil who was taller than most people in the room put his hand up to thank them.

"Crafty sod" thought Trevor.

"As for me, I'm going to be non-executive director of Bright Interiors. I'll attend Board meetings once a month, Joe has a project he wants me to do on some new energy standards and I'm going to be doing regular toolbox training sessions."

"In fact, you lot" David said, pointing to the gaggle of men on one side of the room who were wearing suits for the first time this year, "will probably see more of me than you ever did before!" This was followed by a discernible but good-natured grown from the group.

"But that won't be for at least three weeks. Because Jean and I are off on holiday at last"

"About bloody time, Dad" called out Ruby which elicited the laugh that David hoped he would have got earlier.

Big announcements out of the way, the event continued the way these things do. Guests made excuses to leave and get back to their businesses

Chapter 29

that couldn't cope without them. A newly empowered Phil worked the room, tapping phones with younger guests and exchanging cards with the older ones. Dan found himself cornered by one of the customers who was determined to explain every detail of why his own business was so successful and Joe chatted with the staff while polishing off the chicken drumsticks.

Meanwhile as if magnetically attracted to each other, Ruby, Trevor, Jean and Matt talked about the business, life, accountancy exams and holidays.

"I might have known you four would end up together" interrupted David. "The only four people in my life brave enough to tell me when I've cocked something up."

"Congratulations" said Trevor. "Never thought you'd be able to do it."

"Yep, me neither Trevor" replied David. "I've done laps round this. But the three of them are ready to run things now and build this into something bigger. I won't be too far away if they need me and one of the conditions is that Matt sends me figures every month and tells me about any concerns he has."

"I think we'll be ok won't we Matt?"

"I think it'll be fine David" replied Matt. "I'm confident that the future's Bright".

Next steps

If you are determined to make your business less dependent on you and are prepared to commit some time to the project, then this is your guide. This is the not the order I did it. I did things in completely the wrong order and it was only once I'd done them all that I realised the order in which I should have done it. So pay attention. If you want to make your business less dependent on you, this is the order that you do things:

1. Create an index of roles:
   a. The important thing is to de-personalise the roles. Many of your staff will occupy more than one role (in some cases many roles). You will probably occupy many roles yourself. If you are going to make your business less dependent on you, you will need to imagine your business bigger than it is now. Maybe 50% bigger.

   b. Take the index of roles in Appendix B and adapt to your own business. The sections on Sales and Marketing, Finance and Admin and Personnel and Training might not take much adjustment although there will be issues that are specific to your business and there may be some key roles that do not exist in our generic template. However, the Operations section will need to be designed from scratch

Next Steps

2. Identify which of the roles are Primary Roles and which are Multi-roles. As a reminder a Primary role is one where only one person must ever undertake that role. It is all about responsibility which can be delegated but not shared.

   Generally speaking, anything involving Head of Department, Manager or Superviser is likely to be a Primary role, most assistant roles will be multi roles as will most specialist roles. Remember just because there is only one person doing it, doesn't make it a Primary role, if it involves a pool of work which could be shared if it was big enough that makes it a multi-role.

   Sometimes there will be multi-roles with primary elements. For example, your business may have several account managers who all look after a list of clients each. For each client only one Account Manager is responsible for all the issues relating to that client so in that respect it is much like a Primary role.

3. For each Primary role, appoint someone to undertake that role. Then appoint a deputy (someone who will cover that role when the main incumbent is not available) and a second deputy who will cover when neither person is available. You may find yourself listed as deputy or second deputy on many of those roles but that's ok as long as you are not the main holder of too many roles.

4. For each Multi-role, list all those who undertake that role even if only on an occasional basis.

5. Create a staff page for each member of your team (using Appendix A) listing out all the roles that person occupies or deputises on.

6. Identify a role where much great clarity is required. Using Appendix C, list out all the issues and tasks that this role is responsible for.

7. Sit down with the person (if it's a Primary role) or persons (if a multi-role) who undertake that role and discuss whether the contents of the role page clearly set out everything that role is responsible for. Then finalise the role page.

Next Steps

8. Repeat steps 6 and 7 for each of the other roles.

9. Identify a system which is currently dysfunctional within your business and re-design it using Appendix D as the basis. Remember that each system must only be undertaken by one person in one go. If it can't, then you have more than one system to write.

10. Identify a key process in your organisation that has a major impact on the performance of your business, for example taking on a new customer or supplying a major product or service. List out each of the systems that make up that process and walk through each element of the process making notes about any changes that need to be made to earlier systems in the process.

11. Undertake Blackbox reviews whenever something goes wrong considering whether the cause is because someone hasn't followed the system, someone didn't understand the system or the system wasn't good enough.

12. Identify systems that are currently done by you as part of one of your roles but could be moved to other roles. Document those systems and provide training to the person in the role that this responsibility is to be moved to.

13. Identify roles which are currently occupied by you which could be moved to someone else. Consider what elements need to be documented better in order to move the role to someone else.

Appendix A – Example Staff page
Staff page for: Insert name of individual

You are the Team leader of:
List out the names of the staff members who report to this person

My Primary Roles
List out the Primary roles (i.e. roles that must only have one person doing them) for this individual.

My Multi Roles
List out the operational roles that this individual shares (or might theoretically share) with others.

My Deputising Roles
List out the roles this individual covers when others are unavailable.

Useful Links
- The Organisation Chart – link to the Organisation Chart of the company (if one exists)
- The index of roles – link to the index of roles for the company
- General administration – link to any general admin systems you have

Next Steps

Appendix B – Example Index of roles

Name of role	Holder of role	Deputy 1	Deputy 2
Managing Director			
Operations			
Head of Operations			
Department 1 Manager			
Department 1 Supervisors			
Department 1 Operatives			
Department 2 Manager			
Department 2 Supervisors			
Department 2 Operatives			
Department 2 Manager			
Department 2 Supervisors			
Department 2 Operatives			
Sales and Marketing			
Head of Sales and Upselling			
Sales Lead Manager			
Sales staff			
Marketing manager			
Inbound Marketing Superviser			
Outbound Marketing Superviser			
Referral Marketing Superviser			
Personnel & Training			
Head of Personnel & Training			
Personnel Manager			
Payroll superviser			
Team leaders			
Personnel Supervisor			
Staff Events Assistant			
Fire Safety Assistant			
First Aid Assistants			
Training Manager			
Training Supervisor			

Appendix B – Example Index of roles (continued)

Name of role	Holder of role	Deputy 1	Deputy 2
Finance and Admin			
Head of Finance and admin			
Finance Manager			
Credit controller			
Invoicing Superviser			
Bookkeeper			
IT Manager			
Datebase Superviser			
Hardware and Network Superviser			
Software Superviser			
Data Protection Superviser			
Admin and Premises Manager			
Health and Safety Supervisor			
Premises Superviser			
Cleaner			
Admin Superviser			
Receptionist			
Secretary (ies)			

Appendix C – Example role page
Insert name of role

Main Purpose of this Role
Explain what the main purpose of this role is. Use terms that would explain to the person doing the role why the role is important and what their goals are. This will enable them to make decisions about issues associated with the role even if they are not specifically mentioned.

Specific tasks as part of this role
Lists out all the tasks that this role is responsible for, structured in a logical format based on chronology or group under easily understood headings.

Useful Links:
Set out links to standard documents or external sources of information that the person undertaking this role may need.

Standards that must be reached
Set out an explanation of the standards that you expect the individuals occupying this role to reach.

Who is this role responsible for?
List out any roles that report to this role.

Who is this role responsible to?
State the role that this role reports to.

Next Steps

Appendix D – Example of standard system
(for example) Preparing sales invoices

This task is the responsibility of Insert name of the role

Each invoice should take no longer than insert budget for length of time you expect this to take.

The purpose of this task is to ensure that sales invoices are drafted as accurately as possible in order to reduce the review time required by the insert name of role that will review sales invoices before sending.

This task will begin insert the trigger for this system such as a notification from a colleague or a date (e.g. first of the month). **The process is then as follows:**

1. Select a client to invoice
   a. First step on how you identify which customer you are going to invoice
   b. 2nd step
   c. 3rd step etc

2. Logging in to your chosen software package
   a. Insert link to your chosen software package
   b. Enter your username
   c. Enter your password.
   d. (If you have more than one company) select the correct company

3. Insert process for how you identify the amounts to invoice

4. Locating the first customer that needs to be invoiced on insert name of software package you use.
   a. (If this is the first time you have invoiced this customer) set up new customer on your chosen software package:
      i. First step on how to set up a new customer
      ii. 2nd step
      iii. 3rd step etc
   b. First step on how you identify which customer you are going to invoice
   c. 2nd step
   d. 3rd step etc

Next Steps

5. Produce the draft invoice:
   a. Select sales invoice
   b. Select nominal code
   c. Select department
   d. Insert details of service provided or product delivered
   e. Check VAT rate applied automatically by software is appropriate
   f. Click save or post

6. Insert details of how you produce any other items which are sent with invoices by your company

7. Insert any other steps that you would need to do which are specific to your company's processes.

8. (If the invoice needs to be checked) send as draft to insert name of management role **that does the reviewing**

9. Send invoice to customer
   a. Set out step 1 for how the invoice is sent to your customer e.g. create a covering email
   b. Step 2
   c. Step 3 etc

10. Repeat points 4 to 9 for the next customer that needs to be invoiced and for all other customers

The next step in the process is insert name of next role in the process **and** link to the system that they will follow.

A4G Breakthrough Freedom Programme

You've spent years growing your business. You've had life and important personal events often interrupted (or even missed) due to your business commitments.

You've always thought of your business as an investment, but you don't know how you'll ever achieve a better work/life balance, or actually make it your pension fund.

For those with enough money but not enough time, there are two ways to solve the problem:
1. Sell the business
2. Make your business less dependent on them

The Breakthrough Freedom Programme helps with both. Indeed, making your business less dependent on you makes it easier to sell anyway.

Initially we'll work through an Improve and Grow session to identify how things work right now and flag up areas in the business that can be tackled to reduce its over-reliance on you. Then over an 18-month period we'll work with you and your team to make the changes that will chip away at the things that use up your time whilst ensuring that standards in the business don't drop.

You'll gain the freedom you desire. Your business will increase in value. And you'll have a clear exit plan when you need it.

What's the benefit to me?
- A better work/life balance
- A more valuable business
- A clear exit plan so you can plan for retirement
- Clear, structured roles within your business
- Less stress!

What's included?
Our Business Breakthrough Freedom Programme is split into two packages, depending on your needs and wants. To help you make a decision, we've provided a brief summary below of what's included in both sessions below.

The Programme:

Initial Consultations including:
- Calculation of what level of capital and financial planning will be required to support your desired retirement
- Use of unique business valuation tools to find out how much your business is worth
- Financial Assessment of the business

Strategic planning including
- An interactive session focused on maximising the value of your business and making it easier to sell
- Explore and implement ways to make your business less dependent on you
- Explore and document ways to systemise your business from delegation, role identification and outsourcing
- A detailed review of your staffing strategy levels including optimum

levels, ability and structure to meet the company's goals
- An interactive session looking at your current team, how to keep them happy and how to ensure you get the best from them

Financial Controls and Planning
- An interactive session taking an in-depth evaluation of the existing accounts software suite
- Review and implementation of opportunities for increasing the level of automation for financial tasks
- Set up internal finance systems including recruitment and systems
- Weekly sales analysis and monitoring of average daily turnover

Reporting
- Preparation of your monthly or quarterly management accounts
- Interpretation of your management accounts and how to respond more quickly to the ever changing needs of your business
- Access to and completion of our 5-minute cash flow tool

Profit and Cash Flow Improvement
- Review of your customer service processes from first impressions right through to training staff and obtaining feedback, testimonials and referrals

Ongoing monitoring and support
- Continuous mentoring, management accounts review and updating action plan

The Fundamentals Programme
Initial Consultations
- Initial consultation
- Calculation of what level of capital and financial planning will be required to support your desired retirement
- Use of unique business valuation tools to find out how much your business is worth

A4G Breakthrough Freedom Programme

Strategic planning
- An interactive session focused on maximising the value of your business and making it easier to sell
- Explore and implement ways to make your business less dependent on you
- An interactive session looking at your current team, how to keep them happy and how to ensure you get the best from them

Financial Controls and Planning
- Review and implementation of opportunities for increasing the level of automation for financial tasks

Ongoing monitoring and support
- Continuous mentoring, management accounts review and updating action plan

Is my business eligible?

Your business is eligible if your goal is one of the following:

- To sell the business
- To reduce the amount of time you spend working within the business
- To pass the business onto the next generation

Join the waitlist now
Due to the bespoke nature of our services, we have limited availability on our Breakthrough Freedom Programme, so if you are interested in becoming one of our exclusive clients, please register your details below and we'll get in touch with you in 1-2 working days.

We will go through each programme, where your business is in its journey and your needs and wants and personalise the programme to your business in order to provide you with a personalised quote.

If this sounds like something your business needs, email us at: discovery@a4g-llp.co.uk or give us a call on 01474 853856 to get the ball rolling and achieve a more valuable business, a better work/life balance, and a plan for the future.

References

Armstrong, Jesse. *Succession*, 2018-2023, HBO Entertainment, United States.

Blanchard, Ken and Spencer Johnson. *The One Minute Manager – Increase Productivity, Profits And Your Own Prosperity*, Harper, 2011.

Blanchard, Ken and William Oncken Jr and Hal Burrows, *The One Minute Manager Meets The Monkey – Free Up Your Time And Deal With Priorities*, Harper Collins, 2000.

Bradford City Stadium Fire, May 1985.

Collins, Jim. *Good To Great*, HarperCollins, 2001.

Coppola, Francis Ford. *The Godfather Part III,* 1990, Paramount Pictures, United States.

Founding of McDonalds. 1940.

Gervais, Ricky. *After Life*, 2019-2022, Derek Productions Limited, United Kingdom.

Grenfell Tower Fire, June 2017.

Howitt, Peter. *Sliding Doors*, 1998, Intermedia Mirage Enterprises, United States.

Kings Cross Fire, November 1987.

Lewis, Michael. *Moneyball: The Art of Winning an Unfair Game*, W.W. Norton & Company, 2004.

Liker, Jeffrey K., *The Toyota Way: 14 Management Principles from the World's Greatest Manufacturer*, McGraw-Hill Education, 2004.

Manchester Airport Disaster, August 1985.

Marchioness Disaster, August 1989.

Miller, Bennett. *Moneyball*, 2011, Columbia Pictures, United States.

MS Herald of Free Enterprise Disaster, March 1987.

New Zealand sends military to bolster quarantine facilities, August 2020.

Osgood, Charles. 'The Responsibility Poem', c.1930.

Peters, Steve. *The Chimp Paradox: The Mind Management Programme for Confidence, Success and Happiness,* Vermilion, 2012.

Piper Alpha Explosion, July 1988.

Phillips, Emo. American comedian. Unknown time and date of quote

The Job Retention Scheme, March 2020.

The Killers, "Human", track 1, *Day & Age*, Stuart Price, 2008.

The Watergate Scandal, June 1972.

Thompson, Hunter S., *Fear and Loathing in Las Vegas*, Harper Perennial, 1971.

Walliams, David and Matt Lucas, *Little Britain*, BBC, 2003-2006.

White, Emma. Partner at A4G LLP

To follow

Printed in Great Britain
by Amazon